Making Your Way to the Pulpit

Making Your Way to the Pulpit

Hethcock's Homiletics Goes to the Parish

Jerrilee Parker Lewallen

With Contributions Throughout
and Appendices by William H. Hethcock

WIPF & STOCK · Eugene, Oregon

MAKING YOUR WAY TO THE PULPIT
Hethcock's Homiletics Goes to the Parish

Copyright © 2011 Jerrilee Parker Lewallen. All rights reserved. Except for brief quotations in critical publications or reviews, no part of this book may be reproduced in any manner without prior written permission from the publisher. Write: Permissions, Wipf and Stock Publishers, 199 W. 8th Ave., Suite 3, Eugene, OR 97401.

Wipf & Stock
An Imprint of Wipf and Stock Publishers
199 W. 8th Ave., Suite 3
Eugene, OR 97401
www.wipfandstock.com

ISBN 13: 978-1-60899-068-9

Manufactured in the U.S.A.

The Scripture quotations contained herein are from the New Revised Standard Version Bible, copyright 1989, Division of Christian Education of the National Council of the Churches of Christ in the U.S.A., and are used by permission. All rights reserved.

Appendices and Illustration 1 copyright © William H. Hethcock.

This book is dedicated to Tom Lewallen and Phebe Hethcock and to spouses of preachers everywhere who listen to us with love, encourage our work, and only occasionally say, "That one wasn't your best."

Jesus said to his disciples,
I still have many things to say to you, but you cannot bear them now. When the Spirit of truth comes, he will guide you into all the truth; for he will not speak on his own, but will speak whatever he hears, and he will declare to you the things that are to come. He will glorify me, because he will take what is mine and declare it to you. All that the Father has is mine. For this reason I said that he will take what is mine and declare it to you.

JOHN 16:12–15
THE GOSPEL FOR TRINITY SUNDAY, YEAR C
The Revised Common Lectionary

Contents

List of Illustrations ix
Preface xi
Acknowledgments xiii
Introduction xv

1 Making Your Way to a Focus 1
2 Making Your Way Through the Four Boxes 10
3 Stopping to Consider Hethcock's Theology of Preaching 56
4 Making Your Way into the Written Sermon Script 66
5 Making Your Way Through the "Guidelines"
　　and Finding Your Own Modifications 80
6 Making Your Way Through "Feedback" 94

　　Epilogue How Using the Hethcock Process Can Make Us
　　　　Better Preachers 99

　Appendices
　　A. An Annotated Bibliography of Biblical Resources for
　　　　Preaching 103
　　B. Handout 5: Various Guidelines to Consider in Writing
　　　　Your Sermons 110
　　C. Giving Field Ed Students Feedback on Sermons and
　　　　A Form for Evaluating Sermons 123
　　D. Talking Back to the Preacher: A Manual for Lay Persons
　　　　Who Want to Evaluate Sermons 127
　　E. A Sermon by William Hethcock 145

Bibliography 159

Illustrations

Illustration 1 The Four Boxes 9

Illustration 2 Sermon Work-up Page: A Word Processing Layout for Exploring the Four Boxes on Computer

Illustration 3 A Controlling Metaphor 17

Preface

THIS IS A BOOK for beginning preachers, for preachers who will never have a seminary course called "homiletics" (the art of preaching), for preachers who studied homiletics with William Hethcock and want a review, and for all preachers who are looking for a tested, reliable approach to sermon preparation. In short, this is a book for those who preach regularly or occasionally who would like a clear guide for making their way to the pulpit.

At the School of Theology (SofT), University of the South, Sewanee, Tennessee, the Rev. Dr. William H. Hethcock directed field education from 1979 to 1985 and taught homiletics from 1985 until his retirement in 1997. After retiring, he continued to teach homiletics on semester contracts at the SofT and the Virginia Theological Seminary (VTS). He remains active as a teacher, speaker on the subject of preaching, and preacher.

Hethcock's teaching evolved over many years of working with students. He relies on the work of noted scholars in the field, such as Fred B. Craddock, Thomas Long, O. C. Edwards, Jr., and Eugene Lowry. Assimilating the work of these and other scholars, Hethcock developed his own process for approaching sermon preparation on a weekly basis. This book summarizes and describes the Hethcock method. When followed, his process reliably gets the preacher to the pulpit with a biblical proclamation that resonates with individuals in today's congregations.

As a regular weekly preacher, I used Hethcock's basic approach for approximately ten years in parishes, and I continue to use it where I supply now that I am retired. In this book, I reflect on Hethcock's teaching and explain how I have used, extended, and adjusted it to prepare sermons. Included are Hethcock's method of getting to a focus statement though use of the four boxes (chapters 1 and 2), theology of preaching (chapter 3), sermon script preparation (chapter 4), guidelines for sermon preparation (chapter 5), feedback for the preacher (chapter 6), and a short epilogue reflecting on my use of Hethcock's process.

Significant illustrations are Hethcock's four boxes and my computer layout for working through them. The appendices are Hethcock's annotated bibliography of preaching resources along with my reflections and updates, guidelines for sermon preparation, design for congregational feedback, and one of his sermons.

Though I am a priest in the Episcopal Church, I have written this book as a nondenominational guide for ministers, priests, deacons, sisters, and brothers who would like to use a dependable process for preparing sermons.

Acknowledgments

It has been a delight to work on this book with Bill Hethcock. He has given me access to his unpublished materials and hours of interview time. He has read multiple drafts and worked with me on every section. Since the book began as a project for my doctor of ministry degree, this process has gone on for years. Bill has been consistently generous and patient. His gentleness as a teacher is replicated in his relationship with grandson, Timmy, who often popped in and out of interviews with treats of stories and crayon drawings. I am grateful to Bill's wife, Phebe, for her good spirit and hospitality throughout this time.

I want to thank the Rt. Rev. Dr. Neil Alexander for being the first reader on the D. Min. project, the Rev. Dr. Don Armentrout for being the second reader, and Sue Armentrout for proofing the project. Their help was invaluable.

Since I had never written a book, it would not have been possible to make the project into a book without copyediting by Kathy Hamman. She was not only a copyeditor, but also a writing coach and encourager.

Finally, I want to say thank you to my husband, Tom, for supporting me in so many ways, and especially for brightening writing days with smiles, hugs, and kisses.

Introduction

IN THE SPRING OF 1995, after sojourns as a classroom teacher and social worker and after nearly twenty years of practicing law and being a mother of three, I found myself at a seminary on the campus of the University of the South, in Sewanee, Tennessee. It's known as The School of Theology (SofT), as if, of course, there were no other School of Theology. I was a postulant for Holy Orders from the Episcopal Diocese of Alabama. My husband, Tom, was closing his business in our hometown, and I would soon leave employment at the law firm to take a summer for winding down and packing. We were in the process of selling our home and moving from the town where I had gone to high school and then returned as a fresh young lawyer many years later; where my husband had spent nearly all his life, gone to college, and been in business; where we had married; where my older children had attended elementary, middle school, and high school; and where our son had been born and gone through elementary and middle schools.

We were at Sewanee for preliminary interviews to see if I would be accepted for seminary in the fall. We were making the rounds, talking with the seminary's director of admissions, speaking with administration officials about housing opportunities, looking at St. Andrew's Episcopal School for our son, and meeting some students and one faculty member. Every prospective new student was assigned one faculty member with whom to meet. Professor William Hethcock was assigned to me.

Tom and I found our way to Hethcock's book-lined office on the main floor of Hamilton Hall, an imposing stone structure that had once been a classroom building for the Sewanee Military Academy (SMA). It took me back a bit to be in Sewanee. I had dated an SMA student for a short time and remembered posing with him on one of the bluff overlooks: I probably wore a tailored, late 1950s skirt and jacket, and he, somewhat shorter than I, as I was then beginning to wear heels, was turned out smartly in his SMA uniform. I might even have been wearing gloves. Meeting Hethcock called me back to that time. There was an old school, courtly manner about him. He looked and acted like someone we might have known in those more proper days thirty years ago.

I perceived this as an admissions interview because that was how it was billed. Hethcock knew that even though the process required an "admissions" interview, a student's admission to the SofT was not going to depend solely on that interview. The real purpose of the interview was for the professor to help the prospective student choose an appropriate place to attend seminary.[1]

There was nothing informal about this admissions interview as far as I was concerned. I wondered about my lackluster scores on the Graduate Record Exam (GRE). I had taken the exam after weeks of working with one of those preparation (cram) books for hours each night from Halloween into December of 1994, mainly to avoid embarrassment by my loss of basic math skills. I had even worked on my vocabulary. Law School entrance exams did not count for admission to seminary, and my having been admitted to the bar in two states did not waive the GRE requirement. Years of writing briefs had not done much to improve my performance. To make matters worse, the morning of the GRE happened to be the first Saturday of the evening Nutcracker performance in our hometown. Tom and I had danced the parts of Father and Mother Stahlbaum for years, and this was our last chance, so we had decided to "break a leg" one more time before the seminary venture. That decision did nothing to improve my GRE performance. The interview with Professor Hethcock was the last step in the process before beginning seminary. Because of our family obligations, we were only considering Sewanee, just a bit north of the Alabama-Tennessee border. So, it was make or break. If Sewanee would not have me, I did not have a clue about what I would do or where we would go.

With these thoughts and anxieties rattling in my head, I sat down to face Hethcock, and Tom perched on a chair slightly over to the side so he could be available to join the conversation but not intrude on it. And I began to make my case. Today, I do not remember what that case was. Perhaps I began explaining my problems with the GRE. Or perhaps I led with a stronger hand, emphasizing that despite test scores and a none-too-stellar undergraduate record at the University of Texas, I had done well at law school at Indiana University and gone on to make a

---

1. Interview with William Hethcock, May 30, 2008.

career. The seminary could take a chance on me. I would work hard. Somewhere midway into my oral argument, this gentle man cut through my anxiety with a little laugh. And he told me that the situation was reversed. He was not concerned about whether Sewanee would accept me. My credentials were acceptable to the seminary. My GRE scores, whatever they were, had been approved. I was a postulant, and he was there to encourage me to choose Sewanee as a seminary. Imagine that!

Hethcock later told me that other students also were very anxious during this interview. Billing it as an "admissions interview" was the kind of miscommunication that would add to anxiety.[2] On reflection, I can see that I was learning something about clear communication from Bill Hethcock at our very first meeting.

With a huge sense of relief, I sat back in my chair and exhaled. This was going to be all right. Maybe I should find out something about what this professor taught.

I knew he taught preaching. So I told him, quite honestly, that preaching was the one subject about which I was most concerned. After all, I figured naively, I could count on my previous experience at law school to give me an edge in "academic" subjects. The differences between the head, the heart, and the whole being approach necessary for academic subjects at seminary and the mostly "head" approach in law school would become apparent in due time. Somehow, even then in Hethcock's office in the spring of 1995, I knew preaching would be different. I knew it would not be like arguing a case, not really. I knew it was more art and craft and something intangible. How did one learn that?

Again, piercing my anxiety, Hethcock relaxed into his chair and told me something in no uncertain terms drawn from his many years of teaching homiletics.[3] He told me that, like his other students, when I left seminary, he would have taught me a way into the pulpit. I would know where to start and how to prepare. I could be taught how to convey God's word with a style of preaching that people today could hear. It was a promise he often made to new preaching students. He would say, "If

2. Interview with Hethcock, May 30, 2008.

3. By that time Hethcock had been teaching preaching at the University of the South's School of Theology (hereinafter SofT) in Sewanee, Tennessee, for ten years. Before then he had been the SofT's field education director for six years, and before that had served the Episcopal Church at the parish and diocesan level for twenty years. For a review of his academic and priestly service to the church, including publications, see Armentrout, "William Hethcock," 203–10.

you will do what I say, you will craft a more effective sermon, one that is supposed to do, in less time, what it is intended to do."

Hethcock kept his promise to me that day. To the extent that the fruits do not pay full tribute to his work, it is because of what I have done with that work. For ten years as the primary preacher serving three different congregations, I used what Hethcock taught me week in and week out, when, as the Rev. Barbara Brown Taylor said in one of her works, the next sermon comes along "like the telephone poles on the highway."[4]

The purpose of this book is to describe and reflect upon parish use of the teachings of William Hethcock in homiletics at the University of the South. In writing it, I hope to preserve a valuable legacy of preaching instruction that might otherwise be lost. Hethcock has taught many students over the years. He estimated, when teaching a preaching class at the Virginia Theological Seminary (VTS), that by the fall of 2004 he had heard and given feedback on more than 4,500 student sermons.[5] Former students still tell him they are using the process they learned in his class.[6] I am certainly not alone in this. What I have to offer in this book is my own experience in parishes as I followed Hethcock's methods of sermon preparation. I reflect on how I have used what he taught about creating sermons and hope that those who read this book will try to use this method.[7]

Jerrie Lewallen

The Season after Pentecost, 2010
Sewanee, Tennessee

---

4. One of Taylor's descriptive phrases, source unknown.

5. Interview with Hethcock, June 4, 2008.

6. Interview with Hethcock, May 30, 2008.

7. As with all fine teachers, Hethcock has grown and changed through the years. His class notes and handouts for Virginia Theological Seminary (hereinafter VTS) in the fall of 2004 are different in some respects and may show improvements in some areas over the notes and handouts in the 1996–97 time frame at Sewanee. However, because of this book's reflection model, I will lean more heavily on how he presented the material in 1996–97, as that is what I have been working with.

1

Making Your Way to a Focus

In the fall of 2007, as in every fall, Sewanee's seminary alumni, students, faculty, distinguished guests, deacons, priests, bishops, spouses, and a few Episcopal nuns gathered at Cravens Hall on campus to eat dinner at large, round tables and to dance to the music of Pat Patrick's band from Nashville. Every year, the dinner dance coincides with the annual DuBose Lectures, a series of continuing education lectures given by a distinguished scholar invited by the University of the South. That year the lecturer was Don Armentrout, church historian and longtime professor in Sewanee's School of Theology (SofT). His topic was William Porcher DuBose, the preeminent Episcopal theologian and first dean of the seminary, the individual for whom the lectures are named.

Cravens Hall is a cavernous space with arching, exposed beams over an expansive, somewhat too slick, black and white tile floor. Chatting across a ten-person round table in a noisy room is hard enough, but because the place has the acoustics of a bowling alley, real conversation is nearly impossible once the band starts playing. Armentrout, known and loved for his funny, irreverent comments in class, would steal a sequined beret from Sukey, the Seminary's director of alumni affairs, and begin to dance. The nuns, some in full habit, might be out on the dance floor. The band's music is too loud, and the prelates, professors, pastors, seminarians, and spouses are too raucous to allow for conversation.

That evening in 2007 before the dancing began, Henry Parsley, bishop of the Diocese of Alabama and chancellor of the University of the South, and his wife, Becky, were seated with Bill Hethcock and his wife, Phebe. Time for any meaningful conversation was short. Bishop Parsley knew of Hethcock's work, primarily because at the request of William B. King,[1] Hethcock had come to Alabama to teach preaching to classes of

---

1. At the time, King was the deputy for Ministry Development and Clergy Deployment in the Diocese of Alabama.

vocational deacons, who, in some instances, could be licensed to preach. However, not much time was allotted to teach them how to preach. Their instruction had to be crammed into a few Saturday sessions. Efficient use of instructional time was an absolute necessity.

Knowing this, Parsley turned to Hethcock and asked this question, "In a sentence, Bill, tell me the most essential thing about preaching." Hethcock was ready. He had answered this question hundreds of times before. Paraphrasing and crediting the person most responsible for the "New Homiletic" movement of the late twentieth century, Fred B. Craddock, Hethcock replied without hesitation: "The purpose of the sermon is not to get something *said*; it is to get something *heard*."[2] Craddock's statement had caused Hethcock to think of and to teach his course in homiletics, in large part, as a course in communication.[3]

Craddock's book, *As One Without Authority*, originally published in 1971, created a paradigm shift from the traditional "three points and a poem" preaching, which he identified as deductive, to the inductive style of preaching. An inductive sermon usually begins with something concrete, such as a part of the scripture, a story, an example, or a metaphor that engages the listeners' intellectual interests and emotional involvement. The sermon's route is charted toward allowing listeners to draw their own conclusions instead of leading from conclusions the preacher has drawn. O. C. Edwards, in his extensive volume, *A History of Preaching*, discusses Craddock's significant contribution.[4] Edwards quotes from Craddock's book, *Preaching*: "In the construction of such inductive sermons, 'the sole purpose is to engage the hearer in the pursuit of an issue or an idea so that he will think his own thoughts and experience his own feelings in the presence of Christ and in the light of the gospel.'"[5]

---

2. This is a paraphrase of Craddock's "central discovery," according to Hethcock. Hethcock, "The Sermon as Educational Event," 26, quoting Craddock, *Preaching*, 167: "One basic understanding of the task of the pulpit [is that] the goal is not to get something said but to get something heard." See also Hethcock's Virginia Theological School (VTS) handout, "Various Guidelines," Appendix B, 1. Craddock was Sewanee's DuBose lecturer in October 2008. For audio recordings of the lectures, go to http://theology.sewanee.edu/.

3. Interview with Hethcock, May 30, 2008.

4. Edwards, *A History*, 799–804.

5. Edwards, *A History*, 803, quoting Craddock, *Preaching*, 157.

Hethcock notes that the very title of Craddock's groundbreaking offering, *As One Without Authority*, signals the shift in authority from the preacher to the listener. And he explains how this shift in authority underlies Craddock's move from deductive to inductive preaching, through which the listener's own thoughts and feelings can become the authority in the presence of Christ. In a summary statement on this shift of authority, Hethcock writes:

> Deductive preaching "worked" when authority was external to the self, up through the 1950s and into 1960s. When authority became internal, the nature of preaching had to change. The preacher's deductive "proofs" became inadequate to persuade a skeptical audience. The question became how to preach to a congregation who are testing everything with their own internal filters. . . . Some evidence of inductive preaching was extant before his book, but if his writing is not the birth of inductive preaching, it is its renaissance, and it introduces the so-called "new homiletic." The new homiletic is perhaps best summarized in Fred Craddock's dictum: Preaching is no longer getting something said; it is getting something heard.[6]

Edwards explains that Craddock's work came in response to a 1960s' attitude reflecting "a deep distrust of words and a preference for action over speech" that was "not restricted to preaching but extended to all speech."[7] Both Craddock and Edwards are saying that words spoken by the preacher and assumed to carry authority, in part because the minister or priest was a congregation's leader, lost some of their power during the decade of the sixties. Edwards says that Craddock

> . . . relates this loss of the power of words to six factors, the first of which is that people are bombarded by so many words. The second is contempt for religious language in a scientific age, a contempt that has been extended to language in general. The effect of television on the human sensorium, through which the aural has been replaced by the visual, is another. The crisis of confidence in the power of the pulpit by those who occupy it is a fourth. Closely related to that is the fifth: Christian belief, which had been a part of Western consciousness since before the Middle Ages, is no longer reinforced by the society at large. And, finally,

---

6. Hethcock, e-mail, July 2008.
7. Edwards, *A History*, 799.

talking to people about the most serious issues of life always has been difficult and remains so.[8]

Concurring, Hethcock describes these differences as coming from changes within the American culture:

> Fast-moving developments in culture and church alike were rendering traditional preaching ineffective. In the culture, reverence for authority was giving way to a degree of individualism that undermined the efficacy and integrity of one-way communication. Religion, especially denominational allegiances and theologies, began to be more openly suspect. The prominence of traditional Christianity began to yield to new spiritualities and Eastern religious influence. A glut of information and a fascination with television in every home was bringing people to listen with different ears, blocking out much communication as merely disruptive noise.[9]

Citing television as one of the reasons for the loss of the power of words is even more persuasive now, early in a new century when congregations are fed with rapid-fire images of seconds-only sound bites.[10]

In addition, Hethcock specifically credits major historical developments: the civil rights movement, the Vietnam War, and the emergence of the "death of God" theologians in helping to develop a post 1950s attitude toward authority.[11] "The point I am making here," Hethcock says in one of his lectures, "is not related to right or wrong. . . . The point I am raising here regards the effect of all this on authority in the culture."[12] Discussing the war in Vietnam, for example, he says, "Whether we agree or disagree with the eventually violent objection to the Vietnam War is not the issue here; the issue is what this kind of objection, seen widely as justified, does to the integrity of authority."[13]

---

8. Edwards, *A History*, 799.

9. Hethcock, "The Sermon as Educational Event," 22–23.

10. According to a *Newsweek* article on presidential sound bites, "the average length of each candidate's TV sound bites continued to fall, from a high of 40 seconds in 1968 to less than eight seconds in 2004 . . . ." Dokoupil, "Television," 9.

11. Hethcock, unpublished lecture notes, hour 1, 3–5. Note: Hethcock divides class sessions into hours. Footnote 11 indicates the first class session, pages 3–5 of his lecture notes. Hereinafter, all references to unpublished lecture notes, SofT, are to Hethcock's notes for SofT Middler Homiletics, 1996–97, at the School of Theology (SofT) at the University of the South in Sewanee, Tenn. He also taught homiletics at the Virginia Theological Seminary (VTS) in Alexandria, Va., in 2004.

12. Unpublished lecture notes, SofT, hour 1, 4.

13. Unpublished lecture notes, SofT, hour 1, 4.

American culture, beginning in the 1960s, experienced a major shift in the location of authority, from authority figures to individuals. As part of that shift, when the power of spoken words diminished, preachers, in turn, lost much of their power as authority figures. Craddock realized that the new emphasis in sermons needed to be not as much on what the preacher says, but on what individuals in the congregation hear and how they, in turn, appropriate what they hear using their own authority.

Recognizing this shift in authority, a preacher using induction will construct a sermon so that members of the congregation hear and appropriate one proclamation, that is, one main point. Hethcock's overarching rule of sermon preparation is what he told my middler seminary class: "Do not preach a sermon with more than one point—ever." His rationale: "Two points (or any number more than two) confuse the listener and dilute the proclamation."[14] Noting the firmness of this position, Hethcock writes:

> Why am I so rigid about allowing only one point or theme? A course in homiletics is not merely a course in Bible and theology; it is also a course in communication. Listening theorists tell us that a group of persons hearing an oral communication can hear only one point clearly and persuasively. When the speaker tries to deliver two or more points persuasively, listeners are much less likely to hear any points at all, and in the end are less likely to affirm anything they have heard with their own internal authority. Contemporary listeners are easily confused or distracted by what they hear as overmuch data. I have found this theory affirmed repeatedly by feedback from students listening to and giving evaluation to fellow student preachers.[15]

The one point a preacher aims for the congregation to hear has to be boiled down to something called a "focus sentence." To be sure, Hethcock is not the father of the focus sentence. That paternity is hard to determine. It might belong to Henry Grady Davis, as described in his 1958 book, titled *Design for Preaching*.[16] However, Davis does not coin the words, "focus sentence." He relies on the thinking of a predecessor, John Henry Jowett, who offers his ideas in *The Preacher, His Life and Work*, a book published in 1912. In the following excerpt from his book,

14. Unpublished lecture notes, SofT, hour 5, 4.
15. Hethcock, e-mail, July 2008. Hethcock is not alone in this insistence. For a different approach with a similar attitude about unity, see, for example, Wilson's chapter on sermon unity, "One Text, One Theme."
16. Davis, *Design*.

Davis quotes Jowett's good, detailed definition of what has more recently become known as a "focus sentence."

> "No sermon is ready for preaching, nor ready for writing out, until we can express its theme in a short, pregnant sentence as clear as a crystal. I find the getting of that sentence the hardest, the most exacting, and the most fruitful labor in my study. To compel oneself to fashion that sentence, to dismiss every word that is vague, ragged, ambiguous, to think oneself through to a form of words which defines the theme with scrupulous exactness – this is surely one of the most vital and essential factors in the making of a sermon: and I do not think any sermon ought to be preached or even written, until that sentence has emerged, clear and lucid as a cloudless moon."[17]

It is not easy to achieve "a short, pregnant sentence as clear as crystal" or a sentence that is "clear and lucid as a cloudless moon"; both are good descriptions of what we now call a focus sentence. Davis builds on Jowett's work by noting that Jowett's procedure would make every sermon a series of points in support of the statement or "illumination of the same predicate," that is, "the predicate of the theme sentence."[18] Davis foreshadows Craddock's understanding of the importance of getting material in a sermon *heard*, as opposed to getting the material *said*. Significantly, Davis points out how different it is to make sure something is *heard* in a sermon. He notes the differences between hearing and reading: 1) the preacher is all the hearer has to go by; 2) there is only one chance to hear it because the hearer cannot re-read the sentence missed; and 3) the hearer can rely only on memory.[19] Davis's observations in 1958 precede the more complicated obstacles to hearing a sermon's message faced by today's television-trained, multi-tasking congregations.

In pursuit of clarity as "lucid as a cloudless moon" that modern congregations can actually hear, other scholars suggest how to define and craft the focus sentence. "The *focus statement*," writes Thomas G. Long, "is a concise description of the central, controlling, and unifying theme of the sermon. In short, this is what the whole sermon will be 'about.'"[20] Long spends pages working with focus and function statements, the latter being "a description of what the preacher hopes the sermon will create or cause

17. Davis, *Design*, 37, quoting Jowett, *The Preacher*, 133.
18. Davis, *Design*, 140.
19. Davis, *Design*, 165–67.
20. Long, *The Witness*, 86.

to happen for the hearers."[21] He says the focus and function statements should "grow directly out of the exegesis of the biblical text," "should be related to each other," and "should be clear, unified and relatively simple."[22] Long's book was a staple in Hethcock's preaching classes.

Hethcock offered his students much more than the idea of the focus sentence, how to work with that concept, and the insight that getting something heard was more essential in preaching than getting something said. What he offered was a way to pursue a clarity of proclamation "as lucid as a cloudless moon," so as to allow individuals in a congregation to dip into the biblical depth behind that cloudless moon and to hear something that would make a difference not only in their understanding of scripture, but also a difference in their lives. This book offers a step-by-step description of Hethcock's unique sermon preparation methodology together with his insights on the process and my adaptations of it.

The "aha" moment for Hethcock happened at Sewanee in a sermon listening group not long after he began teaching homiletics.[23] These listening groups would meet in small spaces; chairs for six to eight students circled to face a podium where a student preacher would stand, preaching for the group and into a video camera. Hethcock had trained the students in how to listen and give feedback.[24]

As a visual person, Hethcock listened to students' sermons while taking notes; he then charted the sermons by sections, making blocks on the board, writing the subject of each block, then showing how the blocks were related. "In order for me to work with the sermon you just preached," he would tell the student, "I have to write it down. I can take notes and can usually get nearly all of it. Then I can see what the transitions are in the sermon and that there needs to be a strengthened link. I can do it on paper better."[25] When the student gave permission for him to do that, he would go to the blackboard and begin drawing those blocks.

---

21. Long, *The Witness*, 86.
22. Long, *The Witness*, 86, 88, 89.
23. Interviews with Hethcock, May 30, 2008, and June 4, 2008. Hethcock began giving feedback in sermon listening groups during his time as field education director (1979–85) for the SofT. He started teaching homiletics at the SofT in 1985.
24. Feedback, an essential part of the seminary education process, will be covered in chapter 6 of this book.
25. Interview with Hethcock, May 30, 2008.

Hethcock said, "I would try to show the sermon's opening and where there was a first hint of an introduction, and what developed after that, what detracted and might be omitted, how the sermon developed its theme and moved to proclamation."[26] He would ask if the content of a particular block were weak or strong, if there were language that could be used to strengthen it. He might ask the class to look at a move from one block to the next, and then he would ask how the move affected them.

In the midst of one of these presentations, Hethcock began to see that he had been thinking of his own sermon preparation process visually in blocks—that he could diagram the way he prepared to write a sermon. Becoming aware of his own process in that moment, he realized that it could be systematized, could become a way to teach. He asked himself, "Why don't I use this visual system that we were looking at for the students' sermons to develop a way to look at sermon preparation?"[27]

What emerged is something Hethcock calls the "four-box" process for coming to a focus sentence. He later explained to his students that this method is an "organic process of sermon creation."[28] When the four boxes have been completed, the preacher can frame a focus sentence (and a function statement if desired);[29] organize the material for the sermon using only what is relevant to the focus, excluding what is not; and begin to write a sermon. Only when the preacher knows the main point of the sermon, states it in the focus sentence, and understands how that point was reached will the preacher be able to speak with enough clarity to be heard. Illustration 1, The Four Boxes, shows the four-box process.

In chapter 2, the Hethcock process of working through the boxes will be explained, along with my adaptation of the boxes using a word processing format, which makes it easier for me to work through the Hethcock process week after week.

---

26. Interview with Hethcock, May 30, 2008.

27. Interview with Hethcock, May 30, 2008.

28. Hethcock, unpublished "Introduction" handout, VTS, 2. Throughout the rest of the chapters, all unpublished handouts for students at SofT and VTS will be referenced by their titles without repeating Hethcock's name.

29. When I was in Hethcock's classes in the late 1990s, he taught, following Long, the use of a function statement. He has since de-emphasized that idea and now places more emphasis on the focus statement.

Illustration 1. The Four Boxes[30]

1. Exegesis What does the reading say? What does the reading mean? ↓	4. Proclamation How does the exegesis Step 1 bear upon the here and now human condition identified in Step 3 among those to whom the sermon will be preached? What from the biblical reading will be proclaimed to the people in the congregation to whom the sermon will be preached?
2. The Human Condition There and Then What is the human condition of those inside the text to whom the reading is addressed? What is the human condition of those for whom the book is written? →	↑ 3. Human Condition Here and Now What circumstances in the human condition of those to whom the sermon will be preached are analogous to the there and then human condition discovered in Step 2?

30. This illustration comes from Hethcock's unpublished class notes and handouts from 1996–97 at the SofT. As noted in the Introduction, Hethcock's teaching has changed over the years. The handouts Hethcock used at VTS in 2004 differ from those given to students at Sewanee in the 1990s. Also, in "How can you tell when you are preaching?" and in "The Sermon as Educational Event" (21, 37), he discusses the process in a manner similar to these four boxes but without using the boxes and content in the same manner. I use my own adaptation of and reflections on the four-box process, which I will explain in chapter 2 and elaborate on throughout this book.

2

Making Your Way Through the Four Boxes

On a visit with our eight-year-old grandson, I was treated to lessons in baseball basics. This was not and is not my thing. "For a grounder, you have to move like a crab," he explained, as I somewhat awkwardly tried to imitate him, using my only frame of reference, a ballet move called a chassé, moving sideways. So far, so good! Then he explained how to position the glove, which I held awkwardly in my left hand. If the ball came this way, I was to hold the glove in front of my face, he demonstrated; if that way, palm up for the ball to drop in. I was to close the glove quickly so the ball could not escape. This may sound elementary, but there was a huge difference between our grandson's guileless instructions and my ability to follow them.

Hethcock's process of using four boxes before starting to write a sermon are comparable to my grandson's lesson on how to catch a baseball. The instructions inside the four boxes (see chapter 1, Illustration 1) are stated in deceptively simple language; however, working through the process can feel like I did when I tried to follow my grandson's baseball basics. Working through the boxes eventually becomes similar to the move from the instruction, "Throw over the strike zone," to throwing strikes. When the ball comes, the player will need to move like a crab or not, will need to hold the glove in front of his/her face or not, as the situation requires. Utilizing the boxes soon becomes a fluid thought process with practice, like a baseball player's reflexive positioning of the glove. In this chapter, as I explain how to work through the boxes, I will share Hethcock's and my own thought processes to help you understand how to use this method.

What Hethcock's boxes do is provide a process before the preacher begins to write or prepare the words of the sermon itself. No matter what kind of sermon will be preached (with or without notes, with or without script, with or without props, in whatever style, from the pulpit, from the floor in the nave, or from a stage-like structure by a preacher wearing a wire mike that makes her look like a rock star), it does not matter; the preparation process comes first. This is about substance, not style.

This is an inductive, not a deductive, thinking process. Craddock develops the meaning of inductive as opposed to deductive in the context of sermon preparation at some length.[1] For our purposes, his definitions of the two terms remind us of the essential differences between the two styles of reasoning.

> There are basically two directions in which thought moves: deductive and inductive. Simply stated, deductive movement is from the general truth to the particular application or experience, while induction is the reverse. Homiletically, deduction means stating the thesis, breaking it down into points or subtheses, explaining and illustrating these points, and applying them to the particular situations of the hearers.[2]
> ... In induction, thought moves from the particulars of experience that have a familiar ring in the listener's ear to a general truth or conclusion.[3]

Using Hethcock's preparation process, the preacher will experience the interaction of the various parts of the inductive process and then draw these into a focus. This organic process then leads to inductive preaching. Hethcock used the following quotation from Craddock in his classes:

> The plain fact of the matter is that we are seeking to communicate with people whose experiences are concrete. Everyone lives inductively, not deductively. No farmer deals with the problem of calfhood, only with the calf. The [chef] in the kitchen is not occupied with the culinary arts in general but with a particular roast or cake. The wood craftsman is hardly able to discuss intelligently the topic of "chairness" but [he] is a master with a chair. We will speak of the sun rising and setting long after everyone knows better. The minister says, "All men are mortal" and meets drowsy agreement; he announces that "Mr. Brown's son is dying," and the church becomes the church.[4]

1. Craddock, "Inductive Movement," 43–62.
2. Craddock, *As One*, 45.
3. Craddock, *As One*, 47.
4. Quoting Craddock, *As One*, 50–51, in unpublished lecture notes, SofT, hour 3, 5. In the Craddock quote from Hethcock's unpublished notes, words in brackets are those in an earlier edition that differ from changed words in the 2001 edition cited in this book.

By working through Hethcock's inductive process, the preacher comes to a conclusion about what will be proclaimed in the same way the wood craftsman designs the chair, without much regard for "chairness."

Hethcock shies away from terms like "parts" or "sections" when discussing the contents of the boxes because these words apply more to the sermon as a finished product. Instead, to describe the contents of the four boxes, he prefers ideas like "ingredients," "areas of emphasis," "dimensions," and settles on "components."[5]

I like the word "ingredients" because it reminds me of cooking. The ingredients one learns to work through within the four boxes are not the actual sections or parts that will emerge from the sermon in isolated, sequential form any more than the cake comes out of the oven as eggs first, then milk, then flour, and at last the sugar. Yet, the cake has to be baked following a process. First, you get out the cookbook, then you measure the ingredients, and then you follow the recipe to make the cake.

First, you look at the exegesis box.

BOX 1: EXEGESIS GENERALLY

Hethcock tells his students that the "encounter between the preacher and the biblical text . . . is at the heart of preaching."[6] He discusses this "encounter" after he has introduced and lectured on topics such as the spirituality and theology of preaching. By beginning with the exegesis box to answer specific academic questions, Hethcock is not suggesting that students skip prayerful encounter with the scriptures. Homilists have taught and written at length about the importance of prayerful encounter. Barbara Brown Taylor says her preparation begins "with a long sitting spell with an open Bible on my lap, as I read and read and read the text. What I am hunting for is the God in it, God for me and for my congregation at this particular moment in time. . . . I run the charged rod of God's word over the body of my own experience."[7]

Many preachers use *lectio divina*, a much-honored contemplative way of chewing spiritually on the words of the text. For me, *lectio divina* is particularly helpful if I experience it with a subgroup of the congregation for whom I will preach: the vestry, a Bible study group, or members

---

5. Unpublished lecture notes, SofT, hour 4, 2–3.

6. Unpublished handout, "Introduction," VTS; unpublished lecture notes, SofT, hour 4, 2.

7. Taylor, *The Preaching Life*, 80.

of the church staff. Other homilists understand that prayer and study of scripture are so intertwined as to be inseparable. Paul Scott Wilson says, "Many of my students lament that their traditions do not have a practice of spirituality such as that developed by Ignatius, yet from the perspective of preaching, preparation of the sermon is the traditional spiritual discipline of preachers. It involves regular study, prayer, meditation, writing and dedication."[8] When you study to prepare a sermon, you pray; when you pray with the scripture, you study to prepare a sermon.

While some preachers, "just read the text and read the text and read the text until it says something to them," Hethcock says, "I read the text several times, but I want to go to an authority and find out what Jesus meant in so far as we know. I really do. And so I run that through my filters and decide what I am going to do with it. . . . What if I struggled all the way through trying to come to something out of my spiritual self and then checked it out with an authority and found out it was a mistake? I would have wasted time."[9]

Hethcock explains this approach: "I am not going to say anything in the pulpit that is contradicted by scholarship. At the same time I certainly am going to try to understand it in my own language and my own metaphor. But I really do want to proclaim what the Bible is saying and what the characters, Jesus, John the Baptist, are saying in so far as I possibly can. I guess there is a tension there. I feel free, after I have studied, to use imagination."[10]

Hethcock recommends that preachers, particularly beginning preachers, select one text only, that is, choose just one of the scripture readings set for the day, from which to preach. The selection of the text the preacher will focus on might require the kind of "charged rod" activity Taylor describes. "You may use *two* readings," Hethcock told my class. "I recommend that you begin by only using one. I recommend that you *never* use three." [11] There is good reason for limiting oneself to one reading that becomes increasingly apparent as the preacher understands the necessity of a single focus.[12] Even if the preacher selects only one reading, it may be necessary to pare that one reading down for the

---

8. Wilson, *The Four Pages*, 34.
9. Interview with Hethcock, June 4, 2008.
10. Interview with Hethcock, June 4, 2008.
11. Unpublished lecture notes, SofT, hour 4, 4.
12. See discussion in chapter 1, this book.

sermon's single focus. "If the reading has more than one point or theme," Hethcock says, "choose one."[13]

I find that I preach on the Gospel at least 90 percent of the time. In The Episcopal Church, the Gospel takes the liturgical high point during the Service of the Word. Preeminent liturgical scholar Marion Hatchett, in his definitive work on the church's 1979 *Book of Common Prayer*, wrote, "The reading from the Gospels, the climactic reading, has attracted special ceremonies at least as far back as the late fourth century."[14] Consistent with that history, the 1979 *Book of Common Prayer* provides for the congregation to stand for the Gospel reading, although the congregation sits for the other readings. The Gospel is always read by an ordained person, a deacon if one is present or a priest if no deacon is available. Because the people are standing, they frequently put aside their service sheets, which contain that Sunday's readings, so that they are dependent on what they hear and are not reading along. Some in the congregation may even close their eyes. Frequently, there is a Gospel procession in which acolytes, a crucifer bearing a processional cross, and the deacon or priest who will read the Gospel walk out into the middle of the church. All of this ceremonial reinforces the possibility that the congregation, acting as one body, will open its ears to the Gospel reading.

The sermon is given immediately after the Gospel reading, without intervention of music or prayer. According to Hatchett, this aspect of the liturgy is a deliberate change from previous Books of Common Prayer: "It is to be noted that the permission in many of the previous Prayer Books to allow announcements, hymns, or prayers to be inserted between the Gospel and the sermon has been totally deleted in this present revision."[15] Thus, the organization of the liturgy asserts that the Gospel is the most important reading of the day. This emphasis is based on Christians' recognition of Jesus Christ as "the way, the truth, and the life."[16] The congregation has just heard the words of Jesus or a story or description related to the life, death, and resurrection of Jesus, as read aloud from one of the gospel narratives. In that context, it is difficult for a preacher or a congregation to shift from the Gospel to an earlier reading.

13. Unpublished lecture notes, SofT, hour 5, 4.

14. Hatchett, *Commentary*, 330. Marion Josiah Hatchett served as a professor of liturgy and church music at the SofT for thirty years.

15. Hatchett, *Commentary*, 332.

16. John 14:6a.

Of course, a preacher may choose not to preach on the gospel reading. And the sermon may cover two readings when they can be shown to make one basic point. One sermon I heard landed on the paradox of apparently conflicting claims—one made in the Gospel and one in Paul's letter the Romans. The sermon focused on living into that paradox. Thus, preaching on the two readings was necessary.[17] However, the vast majority of the time preachers do well to discern what one text will say to the congregation on Sunday morning, and, more often that not, the Gospel will be that text.

Before discussing the exegesis step further, let me say a word about keeping copies of the valuable work we do in sermon preparation. I have established a hard copy filing system because I am old enough to remember when carbon paper and a Royal portable typewriter represented the latest technology. More recently, I have lost work that I stored only on a computer's hard drive or discs, and I've dropped my laptop. As I usually preach on the Gospel, I file sermons and all the work-ups I wrote as I prepared them by the Gospels' titles and chapters; each file folder also includes the lectionary reference. Hethcock uses a numbering system that creates a separate file for each sermon with lectionary and year reference (for example, proper4a08; lent1a08). I prefer to keep all my sermon work-ups for one Gospel together so that they will be available the next time the same reading appears in the lectionary. After ten years of preaching, my files now fill two drawers.

Each of my sermon files has a work-up page using Hethcock's system, which I've adapted for the computer. When I begin to work, I simply copy my "sermon work-up" page (Illustration 2) into the file I am working on and then answer the questions. As the years progress, further notes begin, "new for (date) at (parish)." Illustration 2 (page 17) is a copy of a sermon work-up page that I have saved on my computer's desktop. You will see that instead of calling the four parts of sermon preparation "boxes," I call them "steps." The questions in each of the four steps are the same as those in Hethcock's boxes. If you use a computer to prepare sermons, you may find my work-up page easier to use than drawing the boxes. However, if you write your notes by hand and, like Hethcock, are a visual thinker, you will probably find his four boxes (see

---

17. James F. Turrell, All Saints' Chapel, Sewanee, Tennessee, June 1, 2008. Turrell teaches liturgy at the SofT.

chapter 1, Illustration 1) better suited to create as your work-up page, leaving plenty of space under each question.

Hethcock notes, "It is very difficult to learn how to throw away material you don't need when you are preparing a sermon!"[18] In order to stay on focus, learning how to say "no" to that fascinating bit of exegesis becomes quite important. I find that when I have said it to the computer, that is, typed the fascinating insight into my notes, it will not be lost. The exercise of writing it down dulls my desire to include it in my sermon when the bit of exegesis does not fit the focus of the sermon. However, three years from now, when that lesson appears again, that piece of exegesis may prove valuable, so I do not delete it from my notes.

Illustration 2 is the template for the sermon work-up that I use. This adaptation of Hethcock's four boxes into four steps helps me organize my thoughts as I study the biblical text for my sermon. I type my answers to all the questions in the four steps before I compose my sermon. You may create your own copy of this page, save it on your desktop, and type your notes into it week after week.

---

18. Unpublished lecture notes, SofT, hour 4, 4.

Illustration 2. Sermon Work-up Page

A Word Processing Layout for Exploring the Four Boxes on Computer

LECTIONARY FOR:

BIBLICAL TEXT FOR THE SERMON:

(Type out the text that will be the primary text for the sermon, by verses.)

STEP 1: EXEGESIS

    a. What does the reading say?

    b. What does the reading mean?

STEP 2: THE HUMAN CONDITION THERE AND THEN

    a. What is the human condition of those inside the text to whom the reading is addressed?

    b. What is the human condition of those for whom the book is written?

STEP 3: HUMAN CONDITION HERE AND NOW

What circumstances in the human condition of those to whom the sermon will be preached are analogous to the there and then human condition discovered in Step 2?

STEP 4: PROCLAMATION

    a. How does the exegesis (Step 1) bear upon the here and now condition (identified in Step 3) among those to whom the sermon will be preached?

b. What from the biblical reading will be proclaimed to the people in the congregation to whom the sermon will be preached?

Focus Sentence:

Function Statement:

Controlling Metaphor:[19]
(An optional addition)

"Biblical preaching is preaching on the reading," says Hethcock, "[keeping] in mind as closely as possible using the reading for the purpose the writer used it."[20] Early in the preparation process, then, we settle into two questions about a specific reading: What does it say? What does it mean? In pursuit of what it says and means, Hethcock recommends a variety of preaching resources. These recommended resources for seminary students are listed in Appendix A at the end of this book.

BOX 1/STEP 1: EXEGESIS

1a: What does the reading say?

Hethcock explains, "I think 'What does it say?' means to look at the language and especially to look at words that may not mean exactly what they appear to mean." He offers an example from his own sermon preparation:

> I was dealing with Matthew's story of the tenants, and the commentary said the word "fruits" occurs toward the end. "Fruits" is an important word. If you look in the Greek, it occurs up in the beginning [of the story], but it is obscured by both the NIV [New

---

19. The concept of a controlling metaphor, discussed at the end of this chapter, can be useful in preparing some sermons.
20. Unpublished lecture notes, SofT, hour 4, 4.

International Version] and the NRSV [New Revised Standard Version]. Well, it turns out to be a key Matthean term because the fruits of one's life are the fruits of the kingdom. That is what he is using the word for. I think he is using the term—those are the works; works result in fruits. So that would be an example of when trying to find out what it said made me discover that there were some implications in there that were not clear in any of the translations I was using.[21] . . . I try to use at least one verse-by-verse commentary, so that if there are any tricky words in there they show up. Sometimes I use two [commentaries].[22]

As I prepare my sermons, this first box works best for me if I pursue the two questions in it separately. What does it say? I usually begin exegesis by typing the chosen text, verse by verse, into the computer, reading the words aloud (or at least hearing them in my mind) as I type them. The combination of eyes, hands, voice, and ears keeps me from rushing through the words. Then I can ask questions about each verse.

Rebecca Wright[23] is fond of sharing "Becky's first rule" with her Hebrew and Old Testament students: "You cannot know what it means until you know what it says." From only two semesters of Greek, I learned one thing. It may not say what I think it says, no matter what the English translation is and no matter how prayerfully I have approached the text. The example I hold in my mind to remind myself of this phenomenon is the Greek word *tetelestai*, which occurs in John 19:28 and again in John 19:30. According to Fritz Rienecker's research, the word can carry a connotation of "completion." It means "to accomplish" and is used here to indicate scriptural fulfillment.[24]

Back in that beginning Greek class, I recall Richard Smith[25] explaining that it was hard to get at the meaning of this word without over-translating. He said that it meant something on the order of all that God had intended to bring to pass in the work and life of Jesus, which the scripture required to be fulfilled, had now been accomplished and completed.[26] The NRSV, the King James Version (KJV), and the NIV all

21. Interview with Hethcock, June 4, 2008.
22. Interview with Hethcock, June 6, 2008.
23. Rebecca Abts Wright is professor of Old Testament at the SofT, Sewanee.
24. Rienecker, *Linguistic Key*, 259.
25. Albert Richard Smith taught Greek at the SofT for twenty-four years before retiring in May 2010.
26. In an e-mail on February 3, 2009, affirming my understanding, Smith explains

translate the word *tetelestai*, in v. 30, as "It is finished." If, in the theology of the fourth evangelist, the apex of Christ's triumph and exaltation occurs on the cross, this is not nearly as apparent in the English translations as it is in the original Greek. In addition to commentaries, the first time I work up a lesson, I usually check Rienecker,[27] adding anything I find there to my verse by verse notes.[28] And I frequently look at Peterson's *The Message*, because Smith told me that Peterson is a Greek scholar who seems to be able to capture more of the original meaning in his contemporary language interpretation. In *The Message*, verse 30 gets rendered, "It is done ... complete."[29]

1b: What does the reading mean?

This begins the hermeneutical step, the second question in Box 1/Step 1. The word "hermeneutical" means interpreting the Bible. To answer this question, Hethcock relies on others, suggesting that students pay special attention to the exegetical steps identified by Thomas Long in chapter 3 of his book, *The Witness of Preaching*.[30] You may want to practice working through Hethcock's boxes while using Long's steps for exegesis. If you decide to use both tools together, note that the section of Long's book entitled "Moving Toward the Sermon" complements Hethcock's work contained in Boxes 2 and 3.

Hethcock stresses the importance of literary analysis in exegesis (Box 1).[31] He wants preachers to "pay special attention to how the passage is put together, how it fits into its context, and what its writer may

---

further that "*tetelestai*, verse 28 and verse 30, is in the perfect tense, meaning that something "has been done," "completed," "finished." ... The recognition of the perfect tense in one verb (twice) is rather significant in that the perfect tense carries the meaning of something done but continuing in significance. The form *teleiothi*, also in verse 28, is subjunctive, which lets us know that what was promised with certainty, but with no clear promise when and by whom it might take place, ... has now come into fulfillment and finished in Jesus. ... The subjunctive mood in Greek (as in English) speaks to something that is likely to happen or promised to happen but without details as to time, place, person or event possibility. The Gospel writer, or rather Jesus, is filling in the blanks of that subjunctive mood."

27. Rienecker, *Linguistic Key*, 259.

28. For resources for more advanced Greek students, see Dunkly, "Fresh Help," 4–5.

29. Peterson, *The Message*, 231.

30. Long, *The Witness*, 60–78.

31. Unpublished lecture notes, SofT, hour 5, 2.

have intended in his day and time."[32] He suggested to my class that we consider how a 30-minute TV situation comedy is put together. "Look for the reversal. Look in the reading where the trouble starts. . . . As the plot thickens, resolution is sought."[33] Hethcock also advised the class: "Consider the whole reading and consider it in context with what comes before and after."[34] He cautions preachers against using the work of one evangelist to interpret another. Instead, he says to look for what is unique to that evangelist and for that writer's purpose, focusing on the text at hand.[35] Parallels among the Gospels are helpful in this regard, as they make readily apparent which elements of content and placement of text are unique to a particular evangelist. Kurt Aland's edited volume does an excellent job of showing similarities and differences among the Gospels.[36] An example I keep in mind is that while Matthew's and Mark's Jesus talks of picking up one's cross, Luke's Jesus speaks of picking up one's cross "daily."[37] Emphasis on the "daily" nature of cross bearing reflects Luke's particular interest. Because actual death on a cross can only occur once and at the end of a person's life, Luke's use of the word "daily" necessarily makes "cross bearing" a metaphor for how one lives the faith. In the ongoing debate about whether and under what circumstances scripture can or should be heard metaphorically, it is helpful to notice when an evangelist's actual words make no sense at all if heard literally.

Hethcock distinguishes between *exegesis* and *eisegesis*, *ex* meaning "taking from" and *eis* meaning "taking into."[38] He asks his students to consider two pieces of scripture from Mark:

- Mark 9:36–37: "Then he took a child, and put it among them; and taking it in his arms, he said to them, 'Whoever welcomes one such child in my name welcomes me; and whoever welcomes me, welcomes not me but the one who sent me.'"

---

32. Unpublished handout, SofT, "How You Can Tell When You Are Preaching."

33. Class notes taken in Middler Homiletics, September 11, 1996. Hethcock gets the word "trouble" from Eugene Lowry, whose work he teaches from, especially in the crafting of the actual sermon. See chapter 4, this book.

34. Unpublished lecture notes, SofT, hour 4, 4.

35. Class notes, Middler Homiletics, September 11, 1996.

36. Aland, *Synopsis of the Four Gospels*.

37. Compare Matt 16:24 and Mark 8:34 with Luke 9:23.

38. Unpublished lecture notes, SofT, hour 5, 4.

- Mark 10:14–16: "But when Jesus saw this, he was indignant and said to them, 'Let the little children come to me; do not stop them; for it is to such as these that the kingdom of God belongs. Truly I tell you, whoever does not receive the kingdom of God as a little child will never enter it.'"

An example of *eisegesis* occurs when the preacher reads into that text our current cultural attitudes about children: "Children are innocent and unassuming and childlike and childish and cherished and sentimentalized in this culture."[39] *Exegesis* considers the cultural context of the text at the time it was written to take meaning from it rather than inserting a modern meaning into it. "In Jesus' day, children were defenseless. They were totally dependent upon someone to take care of them. They had no rights. They were helpless."[40] Then Hethcock asks how that impacts our interpretation. He offers two possible implications.

- "You must receive me as you would receive someone who is helpless."
- "You must become helpless and defenseless, or realize that state, to enter the Kingdom."[41]

BOX 2/STEP 2: THE HUMAN CONDITION THERE AND THEN

2a: What is the human condition of those inside the text to whom the reading is addressed?

Hethcock invites his students at this point to get out of their heads, involve their hearts, and begin to engage at the feeling level.[42] This is done by looking for the human condition in the text. In the Hethcock system, the preacher will look for an analogous human condition in three places in this order:

- Human condition then and there in the scripture
- Human condition then and there in the community for which the scripture was first written down

---

39. Unpublished lecture notes, SofT, hour 5, 12.
40. Unpublished lecture notes, SofT, hour 5, 12.
41. Unpublished lecture notes, SofT, hour 5, 12.
42. Unpublished handout, SofT, "How You Can Tell When You Are Preaching."

- Human condition in the congregation for whom the sermon will be preached

Box 2, analyzing the human condition of the people inside the text is a critical step in the process. If the preacher goes directly from Box 1 Exegesis to Box 4 Proclamation, and skips the human condition analysis in Boxes 2 and 3, a lecture about the scripture may result, but the sermon will not touch the lives of the people in the congregation. In his lecture, Hethcock would draw the boxes (see Illustration 1) and then make an arrow from box 1 to box 4, explaining that the kind of preaching frequently heard on television moves directly from a piece of scripture to proclamation, without regard to how the scripture has addressed a particular human condition throughout time.

What does Hethcock mean by "human condition"? In general he means, "the situation in which humankind is living at the moment. What is going on? How does it feel to be a human being at this point in human history? What is true about those feelings, and what is false? What are the joys and what are the pains?"[43] Viewed from the perspective of an individual, Hethcock says it is "the state of life in which a person finds himself at a given time; what is going on around him, more than that, what is going on inside him. What is he thinking and doing, and what are the circumstances of his life? Young, old, working, not working. The human condition is in there somewhere."[44] He continues, "Then there are human conditions of personality. Is he stingy or generous, or happy or sad, longing for something that hasn't happened, or having difficulty with the family or parents?" The human condition can be an emotion.[45]

Hethcock considers these human conditions to be timeless. A situation might be "unique and local and particular"; for example, "A factory closes, and people have lost their jobs." But the feelings of "helplessness and longing and desperation" that go with that situation and make up the human condition are timeless. "And for that reason," Hethcock claims, "even though people sometimes say, 'I can't preach to congregations of people I don't know,' you can, because you do know their human condition. You know the congregation, the human condition of most any congregation in middle class American culture, if that is where you

---

43. Unpublished lecture notes, SofT, hour 5, 5.
44. Interview with Hethcock, June 6, 2008.
45. Interview with Hethcock, June 6, 2008.

are preaching." He says that the human condition can also be "fears or anticipations or disappointments or unknown things. It can be the effect of illnesses and so forth."[46]

Then there is sin. Hethcock observes that the state of sin is often what is meant when we speak of the human condition. "The Church and/or the Scriptures indicate to us that the human condition is the state of sin. We are separated from God. . . . I think it is helpful to understand that we sin because we are in a condition of sin. We do not come to the condition of sin because we sin."[47] "Everybody in the world," says Hethcock, "has the same human condition, which is separation from God and eagerness to take charge and be God, so what we're talking about is dimensions of that."[48]

When the identified human condition can be classified as "sin," the result of applying exegesis to that human condition is frequently a challenge to the congregation. Hethcock says, "When you bring the exegesis on the here and now human condition, there is going to be—99 times out of a hundred—a confrontation and a judgment and a challenge to the listeners."[49] However, according to Hethcock, there is a "to know" sermon, and there is a "to do" sermon. When the human condition is a particular state of sinfulness, a "to do" sermon is likely to result. When the human condition is not a state of sin (for example, the human condition of being finite) the sermon's proclamation might be of the "to know" quality. As Hethcock puts it, "The condemnation or the discomfiture or the calling into question is not always that strong, because there is a 'to do' sermon and there is a 'to know' sermon."[50] If the human condition is sin, more often that not the "something" the congregation will be urged "to do" will address repentance. For example, working with Luke 13:31–35, when Jesus laments over the fate of Israel and uses the metaphor of a hen with her brood to show his love, here is a focus sentence likely to produce a "to do" sermon: Christ's loving lament calls us to repent while the opportunity to do so is still present. On the other hand, the purpose of a sermon could be for the congregation "to know" something, usually something about God. There is, however, a paradox

---

46. Interview with Hethcock, June 6, 2008.
47. Unpublished lecture notes, SofT, hour 5, 5–6.
48. Interview with Hethcock, June 6, 2008.
49. Interview with Hethcock, June 4, 2008.
50. Interview with Hethcock, June 4, 2008.

at work here. As N. T. Wright points out, ". . . (since human beings become like what they worship: this is basic spiritual law) . . . ,"[51] when a sermon addresses something "to know" about God, its effect might be to urge the congregation "to do" what it knows about God. Using the same Gospel, Luke 13:31–35, here is a focus sentence likely to produce a "to know" sermon: God's covenant with us depends on God's sacrificial love, yet it is up to us to accept that sacrificial love. Knowing that God's love is sacrificial, and yet it is up to us to accept that love, may urge the congregation "to do" something, that is, to come under the wings of God's sacrificial love. And paradoxically, "since human beings become like what they worship," knowing that God's love is sacrificial may urge a congregation "to do" something else, "to express" its own sacrificial love. Because of this spiritual law that Wright cites, preachers can know that when they proclaim something "to know" about God, they are urging the congregation toward the image of God in that knowledge. Because of this, preachers can make their sermons more gentle, less preachy, less directive, more descriptive, more inviting, and still be effective in urging a congregation "to do" what the preacher wants to urge.

The objective of identifying the human condition is to get to the purpose or theology of a piece of scripture as it impacts that condition. "What we want to do is preach a sermon that addresses the particular theology, if that is possible, of the piece of scripture," Hethcock says. "And when Jesus is talking, he is usually talking about something to somebody, and whatever he is saying is something he thinks they need to hear."[52] Once we have figured out what it is that Jesus wants people to hear, we can, according to Hethcock, infer a human condition from that. "The implication," Hethcock reasons, "is that there is probably a specific human condition in the reading that we are looking at."

In the process of identifying the human condition, it is helpful to start with the general human condition being addressed by a particular evangelist. Turning to the Fourth Evangelist, for example, Hethcock notes, "John addresses the fact that people don't know and understand the Gospel and don't understand who he [Jesus] is. He refers to himself as 'the Light' and 'the Truth,' and the people are living in darkness, and they don't know the truth. You see, that begins to address the human

---

51. Wright, *What Saint Paul*, 138.
52. Interview with Hethcock, June 6, 2008.

condition."[53] If I were preaching from the Gospel according to John, I might name that general human condition *darkness*. Hethcock illustrates with a particular piece of scripture, "And so whatever I've got here on my plate is a piece of that general thing."[54] Hethcock continues with this illustration: "Chapter 9 [John] is Jesus heals the blind man. The blind man can't see. He does not see the light, but as the story moves along, you find he worships Jesus as the Christ. He comes to see the light in the process. So, the human condition metaphorically—I'm sure this is what is intended by the evangelist—is our blindness; blindness is our human condition."[55] If I were making notes for this text, in Step 2 a, I might say that we have begun with the Fourth Evangelist's description of the general human condition of darkness and have moved to a specific example of spiritual blindness. My intention is to articulate the human condition as specifically as possible and to tie the sermon to the text at hand.

Hethcock talks about the human condition using another piece of scripture as an example, Matt 7: 21–29, the Gospel in Proper 4A of the Revised Common Lectionary. He notes that it "opens with 'Not everyone who says to me Lord, Lord, will enter the kingdom of heaven, ...' And it immediately calls up that 'inside/outside' kind of dichotomy that's occurring. People think that their religion and their behavior in worship and so forth are what is called for by the kingdom, but Jesus is saying, 'not necessarily so.' In fact, some people are going to discover in the last days, according to Matthew's wording, that Jesus does not know them because they are evildoers even though they are people who called out, 'Lord, Lord.'" Hethcock goes on to say, "The human condition is the certainty of the validity and power of one's religious belief without listening carefully to Jesus' admonition that we may not have it right." Clarifying further, he says the word "presumption" might work to identify this particular human condition.[56] If I were making notes for this text in Step 2 I might say that the people's presumption that their religious beliefs are correct and have both validity and power may be wrong.

Hethcock admits that his students sometimes come up with human conditions that he has not considered. It is conceivable that a particular text can evoke more than one human condition. "There are times when

---

53. Interview with Hethcock, June 6, 2008.
54. Interview with Hethcock, June 6, 2008.
55. Interview with Hethcock, June 6, 2008.
56. Interview with Hethcock, June 6, 2008.

you are going to find more than one," Hethcock says. "I discovered in working with students that they would come up with human conditions that I never would have seen there. But I think I can accept that sermon and use it to talk about how this student is preaching without being critical of the human condition the person chose, unless I am specifically aware that that cannot be what the Bible is saying. I can't think of an example, but I don't interfere with other people's interpretations if I can possibly help it." Hethcock says, "I am not telling you what to preach; I am trying to help you learn how to preach, which I see as different."[57]

As a student using Hethcock's method, I frequently find that a text will offer more than one human condition. And, I find that it depends upon where I choose to stand in the text and with whom. For example, in Luke 19:1–10, Jesus sees Zacchaeus up in a tree along the side of the road where Jesus is passing. If we imagine we're sitting in that tree with Zacchaeus, one possible human condition that might be addressed is Zacchaeus' wealth. The text tells us that Zacchaeus is rich (v.2). Given Zacchaeus' status as a tax collector and the implications of that role, he represents not just wealth, but ill-gotten wealth. If we stand, however, with those who grumble when Jesus invites himself to Zacchaeus' house for dinner, there could be another human condition. The text implies that these grumblers are judgmental. Depending upon where we stand, then, possible human conditions could include "wealthy" (wealthy as a result of corruption) or "judgmental" (based upon presumed status as not sinful). Given these examples, two very different sermons could result, depending upon which of the two human conditions the preacher chooses to take forward through the remainder of the process. Similarly for Luke 10:38–42, the story of Jesus' visit to Martha and Mary, we might find Martha's human condition to be "distracted and worried," while Mary's could be "in need of intimacy with God." In Luke 18: 9–14, the Pharisee praying in the synagogue could be "self-satisfied or self-justified," while

---

57. Interview with Hethcock, June 6, 2008. Here Hethcock is affirming the more contemporary view of biblical meaning for preaching as he honors the different "human conditions" his students may find. Walter Brueggemann expresses the hermeneutical diversity this way: "Texts are open to many meanings, more than one of which may be legitimate and faithful at the same time. This is evident, in its most simple form, in the awareness that many preachers on any given occasion preach many sermons on the same lectionary texts. While not all such sermons may be legitimate and faithful, many of them would qualify as such, without mutual exclusiveness. Notice that such a polyvalence flies in the face of old-line historical criticism, which tried to arrive at 'the meaning' of the text." Brueggemann, "Preaching as Reimagination," 18.

the publican is "ashamed." Hethcock discourages identifying with Jesus when asking the congregation to identify with various characters in the text. He says, "We want them to identify with the person who is acted upon by Jesus."[58] When I speak about "standing" in the text with someone in order to identify the human condition there and then, we may not be able to identify completely with that condition. We can stand with Jesus in the garden of Gethsemane for the purpose of recognizing the universal human condition of being tempted, and yet, we are not able to identify with Jesus' unfailing ability to resist temptation.

Also, as a student using Hethcock's method, I find that it is important always to do the search for the human condition in the order Hethcock prescribes—text first, community for which the text was written next, and contemporary community last. I believe that this helps avoid *eisegesis* by keeping the preacher from importing contemporary concerns into the scripture before asking first what is the human condition of those inside the text that the scripture is addressing.

Finally, there are times when I simply cannot identify a human condition, and the whole approach seems somewhat artificial. This is true especially for more "theological" texts, such as the "I am" statements in John. When I asked Hethcock about this phenomenon, he admitted to the difficulty and said, "I just keep looking at it until something happens. Sometimes I can't find one, but that doesn't happen very often."[59] I have developed a few ways of looking. One of them is to take my mind off the page of the text and imagine myself being spoken to or in the corner above the scene somewhere watching the action.

Other teachers of homiletics have different language for what Hethcock calls "human condition." Using such language can be helpful. When it comes to composing the sermon itself, Hethcock directs his students to the work of Eugene Lowry.[60] Lowry uses the metaphor of an "itch" that needs to be scratched, another possible way of looking for the human condition. Under the title "Scratching Where It Itches," in his "Your Itch and Scratch Workbook" done for Virginia seminary students to make use of Lowry's work at the composition stage, Hethcock writes:

---

58. Unpublished lecture notes, VTS, hour 3, 7.

59. Interview with Hethcock, June 6, 2008.

60. Lowry, *The Homiletical Plot*. In chapter 4 of this book, Hethcock's use of Lowry's method for composing the sermon is explored.

Perhaps we can see how the exegesis, human condition (then and there and here and now), and proclamation method is greatly influenced by Lowry's "itch and scratch" metaphor. The preacher identifies in the study the human condition addressed in the action and message of the pericope [a particular Bible passage]. The preacher then identifies the human condition in the congregation who will hear the sermon. By the time the preacher reaches the proclamation, the same itch scratched in the reading will have been scratched in the congregation.[61]

2b: What is the human condition for those for whom the book is written?

Once the preacher has identified the human condition "there and then" in the text, the second question in Box/Step 2 is to identify an analogous human condition in the community for which the text was originally written. Hethcock suggests the student ask, "Who was the person, audience, or congregation to whom the scripture was originally addressed? What circumstances or condition existed with these people which caused this scripture to be written?"[62] He draws on a quote from O. C. Edwards, Jr.:

> The most universally accepted interpretation of the Bible today ... is historical interpretation. It asks what the sacred writer intended his first readers to understand. This is to say that the writings in the Bible were not originally set down as Holy Scripture that would be eternally valid, but were originally a response of the writer to a situation that he had encountered. He wrote to communicate an attitude toward that situation. The continuing validity of the Bible depends on there being an analogy between the situations back then to which the sacred words were originally intended to speak and the situations of our lives. If the situations are similar, then we may legitimately expect that there can also be a transfer of the attitude from the ancient situation to the modern one.[63]

I find that this is often the most difficult step because we know so little about the actual circumstances of these early Christian com-

61. Unpublished handout, VTS, "Your Itch and Scratch Workbook."
62. Unpublished handout, SofT, "How You Can Tell When You Are Preaching."
63. Edwards, *The Living*, 13. Quoted by Hethcock in unpublished lecture notes, SofT, hour 5, 11, and in unpublished handout, SofT, "How You Can Tell."

munities. But Hethcock believes the information for identifying this analogous human condition may be inferred from the text itself. "I don't think we know exactly what the people who are listening to Matthew's Gospel being read to them, if that is the way they heard it, I don't think we know exactly what their situation was except as we can infer it from the text itself."[64] This is easier to discern in the Pauline material than it is in the Gospels. Hethcock points out that we know something of the human condition of the people in Corinth and Galatia because Paul is directly addressing them, and their situations are implied in the correspondence.[65]

The task is more difficult when considering the Gospels. Hethcock talks about a clear example of the kind of inference that can be drawn from John 9: "There's a reference in [John] Chapter 9 where the parents of the blind man are afraid they are going to be thrown out of the synagogue, and there are some others like that, not many, but a few. So that's sort of the assumption I take into it from having read about John, that it is written for Jews who are suffering persecution because they are Christians. Even though they are Jews, as Christian Jews, they are not being tolerated in the synagogue."[66]

Using Matt 7:21–29 as another example, Hethcock says that from what we do know about Matthew's community, about its Jewish roots, about the difficulties between the synagogue and the developing Christian community, we can infer the same kind of human condition in the early community that is disclosed in the text itself.[67] This text begins with verse 21: "Not everyone who says to me, 'Lord, Lord,' will enter the kingdom of heaven, but only the one who does the will of my Father in heaven.'" Working on this text, I found a human condition (abbreviated as HC) of "confusion" and proceeded through Box/Step 2, making the kinds of inferences Hethcock suggests:

STEP 2A. WHAT IS THE HUMAN CONDITION OF THOSE INSIDE THE TEXT TO WHOM THE READING IS ADDRESSED?

I want to say that they are confused about what is central in their lives, and Jesus responds with teaching. Matthew wants to portray this teaching in

64. Interview with Hethcock, June 6, 2008.
65. Interview with Hethcock, June 6, 2008.
66. Interview with Hethcock, June 6, 2008.
67. Interview with Hethcock, June 6, 2008.

the same light as Moses' law-giving. HC = confusion about what is central in their lives.

Step 2b. What is the human condition of those for whom the book is written?

The text itself points to a level of confusion because it is clear that those who call out "Lord, Lord" are under the impression that their charismatic gifts (prophesy, proper recognition of Jesus as Lord, healing) are what matters in the community. But Jesus says no, it is how you act on the words I taught you in the Sermon on the Mount. (In Step 1, exegesis, I had already noted that this is part of the Sermon on the Mount.) HC = confusion about what is central in the life of the community.

Hethcock admits that he also brings background reading into his drawing of these inferences: "The Matthean community is largely Jewish and he is writing a document that chooses Jewish metaphor and language. Now, I have to read that somewhere.[68] He explains, "I am not sensitive to it. That requires an awareness of Greek that I don't have and of culture. And Matthew very often changes the message he has received to something that is more special for him. Mark might deal with something, and then he changes it; he deals with it, but he tells the story in a different way. And there usually is a reason for that."[69] Therefore, Hethcock recommends that before each of the lectionary years in which the Gospel is drawn from a particular evangelist, preachers spend time studying that evangelist. He says, "I recommend to students—I don't know whether they do it—that they read a book about Matthew before they start year A. You know—get aware of the background of all these pieces so that when you put them together they make sense in terms of what Matthew's purpose is."[70]

For this purpose I still rely heavily on some of the texts Hethcock and other professors recommended in seminary, a list to which I have

---

68. For an example of one of the places Hethcock might have read this, see the quotation from Robert H. Stein beginning, "Unlike the Gospels of Mark and Luke, which were written for Gentile believers, Matthew was written for Jewish believers." In Hethcock, "Preaching the Kingdom," 165.

69. Interview with Hethcock, June 6, 2008.

70. Interview with Hethcock, June 6, 2008.

added.[71] These texts and others like them may not give me enough information to line up a highly particular human condition, but they do give me enough information to use my imagination and determine the likelihood that a more general human condition exists in that first-century community. Another example of this from one of my own sermon work-ups might help. The text is Mark 8:31–38. I decided to focus specifically on verse 33, "But turning and looking at his disciples, he rebuked Peter and said, 'Get behind me, Satan! For you are setting your mind not on divine things but on human things.'"

Step 2a. What is the human condition of those inside the text to whom the reading is addressed?

The compelling part of this text is Jesus' rebuke of Peter, "Get behind me, Satan." I know of no other dressing down in such harsh language to any single person, let alone an insider, let alone one of the chief apostles. (LTJ, *The Writings of the New Testament*, 164, says that Jesus is reminding Peter of the proper place of a disciple, to follow.)[72] I wonder what the human condition is when we are faced with an angry Messiah, and I want to slice the text right at this point: "Get behind me, Satan." These words were the ones that bounced out to the members of the Bible study group on Wednesday night. (Remember that Peter has already identified Jesus, so he knows who he is rebuking.) In fact, I want to slice the text right before Jesus' rebuke, or right as he is saying it, before Peter has a chance to feel regret or become the least bit remorseful. I want to slice it while Peter is still "ridin' high, fixin' to 'light in a cow dab." After all, the whole scene changes at the cow dab. So, I think I will call the human condition arrogant self-absorption. Peter is over the boundary. He has taken Jesus' invitation to intimacy as an invitation to forget who is in charge here, and he decides that it will be a good idea if he, Peter, "exorcises" (see NIB & LTJ) Jesus of his demonic notions, which involve

---

71. Johnson, *The Writings*; Kysar, *John*; Nickle, *The Synoptic Gospels*; Bryan, *A Preface to Mark*; Wright, *The New Testament*; and Stambaugh and Balch, *The New Testament*. For others, see Hethcock's annotated bibliography, Appendix A.

72. When I make these notes for myself during the work-up phase, I include just enough information to return to a reference and do not bother with proper citations. Here LTJ = Luke Timothy Johnson, 164; OCB = *The Oxford Companion to the Bible*; and NIB = *The New Interpreter's Bible*. Full citations are in the bibliography under Johnson, *The Writings of the New Testament*; Müller, "Son of Man," 711–713; and Perkins, "The Gospel of Mark," 508–733.

the suffering of the Son of Man as a vehicle for God's grace. (Son of Man: messianic term that Jesus himself applies, also human being, parallel to Son of God as respects his humanity, self-definition of Jesus, many other possibilities—see OCB.) HC = arrogant self-absorption.

STEP 2 B. WHAT IS THE HUMAN CONDITION OF THOSE FOR WHOM THE BOOK IS WRITTEN?

I don't know how the Marcan community could have been arrogantly self-absorbed. NIB says that the Roman Christians (if we suppose that Mark was written in Rome) were primarily lower-class immigrants (Jew and Gentile). They are scapegoats for Nero, some under persecution that leads to fraternal betrayal (see NIB, 515). See LTJ, *The Writings of the New Testament,* 158: "Mark . . . uses that relationship [tendency to identify with the disciples] to teach his readers. The message is mainly one of warning against smugness and self-assurance. He seems to be saying, 'If you think you are an insider, you may not be; if you think you understand the mystery of the kingdom and even control it, watch out; it remains alive and fearful beyond your comprehension. If your discipleship consists in power because of the presence of God, beware; you are called to follow the one who suffered and died. Your discipleship is defined by his messiahship, in terms of obedience and service.'" LTJ says that we do not need a group of heretics in the Marcan community to be the recipients of these warnings; rather, we just need ordinary, inadequate human beings to stand in contrast to the paradoxical Jesus. I am not sure what they were doing in Mark's community to be arrogantly self-absorbed, but apparently this condition was there, or at least LTJ thinks that Mark was addressing it.

To show where this kind of thinking might lead, here is the beginning of my sermon based on this text, which starts out inside the human condition I identified as "arrogant self-absorption":

Whenever I have read this scripture before,
  I have always felt a little sympathetic with Peter.
    Why shouldn't Peter object when Jesus
      starts talking about something as crazy as his own death?
        After all, Peter has just identified Jesus
          as the long-expected Messiah.

I thought I might be missing something in the story.
  So I began to think about Peter "rebuking" Jesus
    and to wonder why Jesus gets so upset with Peter.

And that's when I started thinking of Peter
  as a little more like someone I might have known.
    He's a country boy, Peter is.
      I just got back from my uncle's funeral
        a week ago Friday,
          and somehow going back to Georgia,
            touching base with my relatives,
              remembering rural Georgia got me thinking.

My mama was one of 10 children,
  five boys and five girls
    who survived into adulthood.
      They grew up in Fayetteville, Georgia,
        most of them during the Great Depression.

There was Sarah Helen and Annie Doris
  and my mama, Mamie Clyde,
    good Southern names.
      But the boys, Hubert Lafayette and Luther Floyd,
        they had nicknames, like Pete and Buddy.

Pete—that would be Peter's name if he'd grown up
  in Fayetteville, back before Atlanta swallowed up Fayetteville
    and Tyrone and McDonough and Douglasville in urban sprawl,
      much as Jerusalem and the Sea of Galilee
        and all the surrounding towns
          like Capernaum and Galilee
            are swallowed up now in religious tourism.

Back then, country boys were not much at home
   in big cities like Atlanta and Jerusalem.

He's a big guy, Pete is, and quite sure of himself.
   But he's still a small-town boy.

He married a gal from over in McDonough.
   We know that because Jesus showed up in McDonough
      one day and got Pete's mama-in-law
         right up off her sick bed
            just when all the kinfolk
               thought she was a goner for sure.

Pete is a plain-spoken boy with big hands and strong arms.
   When Jesus starts talkin' this stuff
      about bein' killed and all,
         Pete thinks something crazy has taken over Jesus.

So he comes around from his place following Jesus
   and does a mighty brash thing.
      He grabs Jesus by the shirt collar and tugs him off,
         out of hearing range of the rest of the boys.

Pete puts his hands on his hips and sticks out his jaw.
   It's not very respectable for a disciple, no, not a bit.
      And he gets himself right up in Jesus' face
         and he says to him, "What is it got into you, Jesus?
            You done lost your mind to whatever it is!
            You get that craziness outa your head!"

I think that is what the Bible means
   when it says Peter "rebuked" Jesus.
"Rebuked" just does not quite give us the picture.
      Too tame to feel the shock Mark intends us to feel.
         Peter wants to rid Jesus of demonic possession.[73]

---

73. This sermon introduction violates or modifies some of Hethcock's suggested guidelines, which are the topics of chapter 5 of this book, particularly about use of first person pronouns and mention of family. Tied in with those modifications is my decision to use language that could be a caricature in a particular congregation. I once preached a sermon that made a huge thud by use of such language. It was in a congrega-

BOX/STEP 3: THE HUMAN CONDITION
HERE AND NOW

Once we have identified the human condition in the text and in the community for which the text was first created, Hethcock's Box 3 takes us to an analogous human condition in the congregation for which the sermon will be preached.[74] The place to start this search is with the preacher. I find this to be so especially if the human condition can be equated with sin and even more so if the human condition is particularly noxious, as in the previous example from one of my work-ups. The preacher needs to be able to hear the call of the Gospel to self first and needs to be especially careful about being "preachy" to the congregation regarding a human condition. The preacher first must own the sin, must be able to recognize it in him/herself or empathize with what causes that particular human condition. Even if the sin were one the preacher had not actually committed, the preacher must at least be able to access feelings that would give rise to that particular sinful act. For example, while it might not be likely that the preacher or anyone in the congregation has acted out violently, they all might be able to own and recognize the kind of ossified anger that can lead to violence.

Hethcock writes of this necessity: "In order to accomplish this more consequential preaching, preachers must have examined themselves and found where the Gospel has touched their personal experience and informed their personal pulpit witness."[75] And he quotes O. C. Edwards,

---

tion composed mostly of transplants to the South, drawn to suburban homes planted in former cotton fields by the lure of good jobs with government contractors. It was a sermon on the parable of the man who had two sons (Luke 15:11–31). I named the older son Bubba, which would have been fine in a small southern town, where Bubba could be the name of an older brother or a cousin, now a successful restaurateur or entrepreneur of some sort. But in the congregation where I was preaching, the name Bubba only brought up visions of *Hee Haw*, the television comedy series. However, I preached the sermon quoted above in a small southern town where most folks knew a Bubba and where my use of the first person pronoun and family references served to give me the grounding in language we had all heard and would recognize as a shocking way for Peter to talk to Jesus.

74. See footnote to Illustration 1, where I explain that I am relying on the composition of the boxes as Hethcock used them at the SofT in 1996–97. When Hethcock taught homiletics at VTS in 2004, the composition of the boxes differed. At VTS in his course handout, he did not include a search for "a human condition then and there in the early community" as a separate question in Box 2. However, I consider this separate inquiry about the early community especially important in giving the sermon depth.

75. Hethcock, "'Crossing the River," 149. This article and "the more consequential

Jr., on the same point: "Preaching is sharing the deepest and most urgent things we know to say. This means that the text must speak to the preacher before it can speak through the preacher to anyone else. We have to be the first hearer of all our sermons. I'm sure many of you have discovered as I have that when we preach most directly to ourselves, we are most likely to reach others as well."[76]

If we preachers locate inside ourselves the identified human condition in some specific manner, it will be much easier to craft a sermon that speaks "most directly to ourselves" so that it will be "most likely to reach others as well." Fortunately or unfortunately, I find that it is usually not difficult to identify the human condition in myself, though it might be a painful admission, and paradoxically, therein lies the difficulty. One week I even wrote in my work-up, "I hate it when I pick one of these negative human conditions because I always have to own it first myself before I dare look to see if it exists in the congregation!"

Hethcock teaches that the search for the human condition here and now is guided by the question, "What is the circumstance or situation present in this congregation that is analogous to the circumstance or situation being addressed by the text?"[77] In his classes, he lectures about the priest's responsibility to understand the human condition. "You and I, if we are to be priests, *must* have an understanding of the human condition (or dilemma). We cannot function without it. We must have a sufficiently realistic and sophisticated view of the human dilemma to identify how it impinges upon all of us *and* how it impinges on the person with whom we are speaking and living at the moment. We must see its transcendence and its particularization. We must see how the latter points to the former, and how the former explains the latter."[78]

Working again with Matthew 7:21–29, I asked Hethcock if he could look in a congregation for the human condition he had identified. He had described the human condition found "then and there" in the text and in the Matthean community as a kind of presumptuousness, "the certainty of the validity and power of one's religious belief" or, to put it differently, "the possibility of persons who are very, very religious actu-

---

preaching" it encourages is the subject of chapter 3 of this book.

76. O. C. Edwards, Jr., at a clergy retreat presentation, February 11–13, 2001, as quoted by Hethcock in "'Crossing the River,'" 149.

77. Unpublished lecture notes, VTS, hour 1, 6.

78. Unpublished lecture notes, SofT, hour 5, 7.

ally not being in touch with God as strongly as they think they are."[79] My question to Hethcock then became, "So now that we've identified that human condition in two places, how do we find it in the third place, in the congregation?" And he answered, "Well, you don't find it exactly. There isn't any way to interview everybody there to find out the level of their personal spiritual knowledge and commitment. There is no way to know that specifically. But my suspicion, as a priest and pastor, is that everyone runs the risk of assuming that his spiritual habits are adequate. I go to church every Sunday. I belong to some committees. I give generously. I make my communion, and I say the creed. But, what if Jesus is saying to me, 'Not everyone who says to me 'Lord, Lord'—so it is incumbent on me to look at myself."[80]

When I asked Hethcock if, in effect, we are "carting over" the human condition from then and there to here and now in order to look for an analogous situation, he corrected my verb. "It would be easier," he said, "rather than carting it over there, remembering it and having it in your mind, go over and think about the people you know and the congregation you are going to talk to, and see if you see anything that is touching each other. See if you see any things in the congregation that are touching the human condition that you have identified. If you sort of think through the congregation with the axiom or metaphor that you have in mind, you find out where they touch."[81]

Here are a couple of examples of my own search for the human condition here and now. In Proper 22 A for Matt 21:33–43, the parable of the vineyard, I identified "possessiveness" as the human condition.

STEP 3. WHAT CIRCUMSTANCES IN THE HUMAN CONDITION OF THOSE TO WHOM THE SERMON WILL BE PREACHED ARE ANALOGOUS TO THE THERE AND THEN HUMAN CONDITION DISCOVERED IN STEP 2?

It is stewardship time, and this Sunday we have our stewardship luncheon, and pass out our stewardship meditation booklets and our pledge cards. The HC parallel could not be clearer at this time of year. We are most possessive about our stuff, whatever it is—our money, our power, our time, our abilities, our accomplishments, our rectitude, our land, whatever. What am I most possessive about? I am most possessive about my

---

79. Interview with Hethcock, June 6, 2008.
80. Interview with Hethcock, June 6, 2008.
81. Interview with Hethcock, June 6, 2008.

authority, my ability to direct my life in the direction that I want it to go. What about those to whom the sermon will be preached? Lots of them are possessive about money when it comes to stewardship. They resist making the commitment of a pledge and absolutely resist the tithe.

In Proper 24A for Matt 22:15–22, when Jesus talks about the coin bearing Caesar's image, I identified "labeled" as the human condition because that is what I thought the Pharisees wanted to do to Jesus, "label" him, or put him into a category by testing him with an either/or trick question.

Step 3. What circumstances in the human condition of those to whom the sermon will be preached are analogous to the there and then human condition discovered in Step 2?

I think we face the same kind of thing today, especially in the Episcopal Church. The culture wants to put its labels on us, such as "pro-choice, pro-life, liberal, conservative, dove, hawk," and so on. Politicians and others with agendas want us stamped into a lifeless, controllable image, one that can be reduced to a bumper sticker.

Again, this time with regard to the human condition here and now, there is similarity between the way Hethcock proceeds and the recommendations of Lowry. Lowry discusses the need for "diagnosis" as being "central to our homiletical task."[82] Hethcock picks up this quotation and others regarding the "discrepancy," "bind," or "particularized problem"[83] being addressed by the sermon and includes those quotes in his "Your Itch and Scratch Workbook" and then comments:

> I think that *diagnosis* is like unfolding *the here-and-now human condition*, a situation in the experience of the listeners to the sermon which is like the situation unfolded in the reading. Lowry is correct in pointing out that for this human condition to be crucial, it must include a human bind, dilemma, trouble, anxiety, or tension. The presence of this bind clearly played out in the human condition constitutes the difference between a good sermon and a very good or excellent sermon.[84]

---

82. Lowry, *The Homiletical Plot*, 41.
83. Lowry, *The Homiletical Plot*, 40.
84. Unpublished handout, VTS, "Your Itch and Scratch Workbook."

In a sermon annotated for his VTS class in 2004, Hethcock shows how the human condition here and now lines up with the human condition then and there by diagnosing the similarity of the bind, the trouble, or the dilemma being played out in both time frames. The text is the Gospel from Proper 8B (Revised Common Lectionary), Mark 5:21–43, in which both a woman with a hemorrhage and Jairus, a synagogue leader with a dying daughter, approach Jesus for healing. Hethcock calls the human condition then and there in the text "a problem of faith." He gets at this human condition by noticing the faith that is propelling the woman and Jairus, in contrast with the apparent lack thereof among others on the scene. He dismisses other potential candidates for the human condition by explaining to the congregation that "the pathos, the drama, the agony, the power of these two situations may be getting in the way of our seeing what's happening. The nameless woman with the hemorrhage and Jairus, the little girl's dad, somehow have faith. The anxiety and humiliation of the woman and the grief and dread of the father are such strong moments here that we do not easily see what the story is about. This is a story about faith."[85] Indeed, when I did my work-up for this sermon, I was drawn by these "strong moments" in the text and found a human condition of "desperation." But Hethcock is suggesting here that the human condition is deeper than what seems immediately apparent.

When Hethcock takes his then and there human condition, "a problem of faith," into the here and now for an analogous human condition, he finds a subtle difference. The human condition here and now becomes "a misunderstanding of faith." He describes that human condition to the congregation:

> This is where some people misunderstand and get into serious trouble. Everyone here has heard horror stories about well-meaning Christians who appear at the bedside of the sick child and urge grieving and frightened parents merely to believe. These pseudo-experts advise the parents that they must have a very strong faith. 'Just believe, and death will not come,' they say. 'That's what the Bible tells us,' they recite. But death does come, and they must then exonerate themselves and they must exonerate God by saying to the parents, 'Well, of course, you just didn't believe enough. The child died because your faith wasn't strong enough.' Such an understanding of faith perpetrates a cruel hoax. This story is about faith, but such a misunderstanding of faith

---

85. Unpublished handout, VTS, "An Annotated Sermon."

as that brings a misunderstanding of the story and a misunderstanding of God's ways.[86]

Now that we have completed an exegesis and identified an analogous human condition in three places—then and there in the text, then and there in the early community first hearing the text, and here and now in the congregation for whom the sermon will be preached—the work is done to get to the next box.

BOX/STEP 4: PROCLAMATION

At this point we begin to address two questions: How does the Exegesis of Box/Step 1 bear upon the human condition here and now, identified in Box/Step 3, among those to whom the sermon will be preached? What from the biblical reading will be proclaimed to the people in the congregation to whom the sermon will be preached? (See Illustration 2.)

It is important to note that we are *not* going to bring our exegesis to bear on the "there and then" human condition identified in Box/Step 2. Doing that would leave us in the biblical text or in the first century, and the people in the congregation would not identify with the proclamation. At this point in our pre-sermon preparations, we must hope and pray that the work we've done has been based in faith and good scholarship, that we indeed have made a valid connection between the human condition there and then and the human condition here and now, so that our application of the exegesis will be consistent with the evangelist's purposes for the text. And at this point, we can more easily see which parts of the exegesis are going to apply to the here and now human condition and, therefore, be relevant to the proclamation; the remaining parts of our notes for the exegesis, no matter how intriguing they might be, are best left for another sermon. I find that the questions in the boxes work best when they are answered in sequence. Only after I discover the connection between the human condition here and now and the exegesis can I decide what my sermon will proclaim.

---

86. Unpublished handout, VTS, "An Annotated Sermon."

> *4 a: How does the exegesis (Step 1) bear upon the here and now condition (identified in Step 3) among those to whom the sermon will be preached?*

In a quote Hethcock highlights for his students, Long explains the essence of biblical preaching: "Bearing witness to the gospel means engaging in serious and responsible biblical preaching. Preaching is biblical whenever the preacher allows a text from the Bible to serve as the leading force in shaping the content and purpose of the sermon. More dynamically, biblical preaching involves telling the truth about—bearing witness to—what happens when a biblical text intersects some aspect of our life and exerts a claim upon us."[87]

Using Hethcock's system, in order for that intersection and that claim to be identified, the preacher matches up the human condition here and now with exegesis of the text. To some extent, making this connection is an intuitive process. It may just occur. And when it does, the preacher should stop in the moment to appreciate that gift. Hethcock describes such a moment, beginning with the exegesis: "I do sit at the computer and type. And I try to use at least one verse by verse commentary, so that if there are any tricky words in there, they show up. Sometimes I use two [commentaries]. And after I have done that, then I can go on to the human condition part and begin to ask what is going on in here. And usually somewhere along in that process, something will light my fire, and then I stop and see if that will work because you should not pass the moment of deciding what really is important to you. You don't want to pass the moment and then go to something else because you may lose that moment, and why do more work if you have already done your work?"[88]

Failing such a moment, however, the preacher may need to look more carefully. For example, in an article for *Homily Service*, Hethcock deals with the Gospel for Proper 28A, Matt 25:14–30, in which Jesus tells the story about the master who goes on a journey and leaves his servants to manage property, one entrusted with five talents, another with two, and another with one.[89] In the exegesis portion, Hethcock answers the

---

87. Long, *The Witness*, 48.

88. Interview with Hethcock, June 6, 2008.

89. Hethcock, "Serving the Word," 34–36, a section within the commentary for November 14, 1993, in Young, Petrenko, Tarker, and Hethcock, *Homily Service*. Note: Though several contributors are listed for this article, the "Serving the Word" section is

question "What does it say?" in part by explaining that a talent "was a weight of valuable metal, a sum of money."[90] Acknowledging what we already know, that talent in the modern lexicon means "gifts and abilities," Hethcock observes that "our talents are like money and wealth to us."[91] And then he addresses the easy application of the parable:

> Making the most of what we have is a familiar focus for today's parable; that interpretation, however, can become tainted with North American culture, even with a little flag waving. Only a few steps, then, to justifying our profit incentive and "how good business is good for all of us." Suddenly, without warning, such thinking seduces us into a self-serving interpretation of the parable that endorses our national acquisitiveness. Thing-oriented people stockpile more things, and moneymaking people invest wisely for maximum gain. That's the American way.[92]

If the preacher had moved directly from "What does it say?" to an application here and now, this might have been the proclamation. There is, however, another bit of exegesis. In asking the question, "What does it mean?" the preacher explores the reason for this parable. "Matthew is not talking about profit motive or investment savings; he is talking about the kingdom of heaven and what it's like (25:1)," Hethcock says.[93] Making that observation requires setting the parable in context and noticing the development of Matthew's theme. "Throughout his gospel Matthew shows us how Jesus labored through parable after parable, metaphor after metaphor, symbol after symbol, to explain what that heavenly kingdom is like. It is urgent for his listeners to understand, for the kingdom is 'at hand' here and now, ready to break in among us, ready to sweep us up into its own special life, its own special way of being in the world, if we will recognize its immediacy and urgency."[94]

Hethcock has now done deeper exegesis and has identified the human condition being addressed by the parable there and then in the text. The human condition has more to do with the urgency of being ready for the kingdom, which is breaking in among the people, than

---

Hethcock's contribution.
90. Hethcock, "Serving the Word," 34.
91. Hethcock, "Serving the Word," 34.
92. Hethcock, "Serving the Word," 35.
93. Hethcock, "Serving the Word," 35.
94. Hethcock, "Serving the Word," 36.

with the need for financial security. By the time Matthew's community had heard this parable, they would have become weary of anticipating the kingdom to come because they had been expecting it for many years. The need to be ready for the kingdom would need to be re-emphasized and re-energized, and that human condition continues to pertain here and now. Surely by now we have lost sight of the urgency; surely by now our own need to be ready for the kingdom that is breaking in on us is even greater.

Hethcock then matches up the here and now human condition, one that resonates with the human condition there and then (the need to be ready for the kingdom that is breaking in), with an exegetical insight that emphasizes the "at handness" of the kingdom that Jesus proclaims. Hethcock says, "When women and men invest their very selves in the kingdom, risking moving out assertively to do God's good work in the world, the result is dividends of the biblical proportion Matthew predicts, letting us glimpse once again the kingdom's 'at handness.'"[95]

4 b: What from the biblical reading will be proclaimed to the people in the congregation to whom the sermon will be preached?

It might appear that the proclamation is in place once the exegesis has been applied to the here and now human condition. And, indeed, it might be. But look at what Hethcock did with the insight cited above. He makes some excellent observations:

> We glimpsed the kingdom of heaven when neighbors drew together in the Mississippi Valley disasters of last summer [1993] to fight the river and to protect each other's well-being. The kingdom is at hand when men and women risk standing by the dying in Christ's name in hospices and AIDS care centers. We see the kingdom when congregations hear the cry for justice and invest themselves in changing systems that discriminate against powerless minorities. In a more subtle way, the kingdom is at hand when women and men risk their talents to live out faithfully the message of the gospel to uphold integrity in the home and the work place, to guide their children into faith and personal holiness, helping the climate of righteousness and mutual concern to prevail over personal gain and safety.[96]

95. Hethcock, "Serving the Word," 36.
96. Hethcock, "Serving the Word," 36.

And now, from those observations of what it looks like when men and women today take the exegesis and apply it to the here and now human condition, Hethcock arrives at a proclamation that is full of the kind of urgency about which he has been speaking: "Look at what talents we have! Not only are they God-given and precious, they are powerful. We dare not bury them in the earth, for miraculously and wonderfully, the kingdom is at hand, and our talents are God's tools to make it known."[97]

We have made our way through the boxes now. We have arrived at a proclamation that is grounded in the biblical text from which it originated and applicable to the congregation for whom we are preparing a sermon.

What remains is to take that proclamation and hone it down to a single sentence that will serve as a destination, keep us on one path, and guide the sermon into being.

CRAFTING THE FOCUS SENTENCE

We began this chapter with Hethcock's description of the content of the boxes as "components" or "areas of emphasis," more fluid and less segregated and sequential than "parts" or "sections." I said I preferred "ingredients" because I like cooking metaphors.

Can you make a roux? As in, "Who's your mama? Are you Catholic? And, can you make a roux?" My father used to make roux and put it away in the refrigerator in little tin cups covered over with plastic wrap. They looked like they belonged in a child's play kitchen. There they would sit toward the back, behind the milk and the sweet pickles, waiting for his next creation. I'm not much good at roux-making myself. Maybe it comes from being an Episcopalian from Alabama instead of Roman Catholic from Louisiana. Nevertheless, I understand the idea that a good dish can contain a critical, cooked-down substance that must be in place before anything else can be added.

After I have written out several sentences describing what I hope to proclaim in a sermon, it is time to cook it down. All we want is one essence. All we want is to achieve a single statement that will be the underlying support for the sermon, the point from which everything will flow and with which everything will be consistent. I take the proclamation paragraph and cook it down by pulling out words and phrases

---

97. Hethcock, "Serving the Word," 36.

until only the essence remains in a single sentence. With each stir of the pot, I am asking myself, "Can this be said more simply? Is this phrase repetitive? Has this thought already been covered?" At the end of the process, I hope to have created a sentence that expresses one and only one thought to guide the sermon.

This takes us back to Hethcock's overarching rule of sermon preparation: "Do not preach a sermon with more than one point ever." As he explains, it is this rule that most ensures a sermon will be heard and absorbed: "According to our best communications theory as it applies to pulpits, part of getting a sermon heard involves making only one point. In order for the congregation to receive that one point experientially . . . the point must be clear and direct, uncontaminated by any material that detracts from the central theme. . . . Experience in the classroom shows us that sermons that attempt to make more than one point lose their strength and very seldom manage to make any point at all."[98]

Here are two examples of the move from proclamation to focus sentence from my own work-ups:

- Proper: Advent 2C, Luke 3:1–18 (John appears in the wilderness.)

Proclamation: This is no matter of confession of private wrongdoing, but a call to a whole social system, and everyone who benefits from it, to have the courage to turn the system around. John's call for repentance at the beginning of Advent makes sense only because it is eschatological [about final judgment] and, as such, demands the wholesale turning around of our way of living.

Focus Sentence: The Baptism of Repentance challenges not just a few sins but our whole way of living as a society.

- Proper 5C, Luke 5:1–11 (The unexpected catch of fish.)

Proclamation: When we know we are standing in the presence of Christ, even though it is a sin-exposing, self-exposing experience, we become aware of who we are to Christ. We are those Christ has asked and empowered to bring others to him.

Focus Sentence: In the sin-exposing, self-exposing, terrifying presence of God, we become aware of ourselves as the very people Christ has asked and empowered to bring others to him.

---

98. Hethcock, "The Sermon as Educational Event," 27.

Hethcock might not describe his process as "cooking down." But he does describe a process of elimination, saying,

> My notes, which I throw away, might have four or five focus sentences until I get to the one that feels right. And when I have done that if I am satisfied with the focus sentence, I quit and start figuring out how I am going to write the sermon, because you only mess up your mind if you continue to struggle after you have found what you want to talk about. . . . They [the four or five focus sentences] would all be versions of the same thing. I am just trying to get it, if I may use the term, "right." Right would be for me in terms of being comfortable with it and ready to use it.[99]

When I ask, "What does it look like when it is 'right?'" he replies, "Well, it is a complete sentence. It may have one subordinate clause. It always has an active verb, never the verb 'to be.' The verb 'to be' is weak in focus sentences: 'The love of God is abroad.' That would not be a very good focus sentence. 'The love of God spreads itself abroad in order to affect whatever.' That is not a very good example, but there has to be some movement in the focus."[100]

When I ask, "Is it always a declarative sentence?" he replies, "Yes. Yes. Interrogative sentences don't work. If you ask a question as a focus sentence, it will not help guide you when you get down in the sermon and say, 'Gee, I don't know what to say next,' and you go back and you have a question up there; then you've got one in your head, too, and they just won't work. It's got to be a declarative sentence."[101]

As mentioned in chapter 1, Hethcock makes no claim to creating the notion of the focus sentence or even to defining the focus sentence and its function. To help students understand it, he directs them to the work of Long.[102] Hethcock synthesizes this concept succinctly in a handout for VTS: "A focus sentence is a simple sentence which will state what the proclamation in the sermon will have said when the sermon is over. The focus sentence reminds the preacher throughout the crafting of the sermon where the sermon is going, what it will have said when the

---

99. Interview with Hethcock, June 6, 2008.
100. Interview with Hethcock, June 6, 2008.
101. Interview with Hethcock, June 6, 2008.
102. See especially Long, *The Witness of Preaching*, 86–91.

preaching has ended."[103] After hearing sermon feedback from students who try to articulate the preacher's focus, Hethcock clarifies the definition and purpose of a sermon's focus sentence in another VTS handout:

1. A focus sentence is short, but it may be a compound sentence or it may have an independent clause. It may be a verse from the reading, but it will serve the preacher better as a focus if it is reworded with his/her emphasis clear.

2. A focus sentence must be a complete sentence. If it has no verb, it will not function as a guide to the sermon. The verb serves the focus better if it is an action verb rather than the verb 'to be.'

3. A focus sentence is *always* a declarative sentence; it is *never* a question.

4. The focus sentence *always* informs the proclamation. A listener should be able to hear the focus in the last few sentences of the sermon, which are designed to leave listeners with the focus in their minds. Indeed, the focus may be the *last sentence itself*. The focus of the sermon should be 'the tune we can whistle' when the sermon ends. All that has preceded it moves toward this point.[104]

Paradoxically, it is not necessary for the focus sentence actually to be *in* the sermon.[105] The focus may be achieved without saying it as a statement, leaving the congregation to hear the focus in their own minds, in their own words. Nevertheless, Hethcock insists his students write a focus sentence. He maintains that the existence of the focus sentence helps the preacher avoid diversions, which sometimes result in a sermon that sounds like two sermons in one. He says, "The best developed sermon moves on one track, developing one point toward one conclusion. This will invite listening from a community of contemporary men and women who are unable in this day to concentrate in an oral communication on more than one subject at a time."[106] A previously written focus sentence "will identify where the sermon is 'going,' and it will hold the sermon on the pre-determined 'track,' insuring the greatest possible hearing and highest level of desired response from the congregation."[107] A good example of a

103. Unpublished handout, VTS, "Guidelines for Writing Focus Sentences."
104. Unpublished handout, VTS, "A Little More About Focus Sentences."
105. My notes from SofT lecture by Hethcock, Sept. 11, 1996.
106. Unpublished lecture notes, SofT, hour 6, 4.
107. Unpublished lecture notes, SofT, hour 6, 4.

focus sentence is the following one for a sermon Hethcock preached at the Church of the Holy Spirit, in Alabaster, Alabama, for Epiphany 3C, from Luke 4:14–21: "Our mission is to hear Jesus' claim about himself and to make it known among ourselves and beyond."[108]

FROM LONG: THE OPTION OF A FUNCTION STATEMENT

The function statement, a sermon preparation tool that differs from a focus sentence, is a contribution made by Thomas Long. Hethcock used it when he taught at the SofT but has since abandoned it as a requirement because he says too many students found it confusing. "Students spend a whole lot of time trying to catch on," Hethcock told me. "I don't think it is difficult at all. After you have said what this sermon is about, then you ask [yourself] what you want the sermon to do." However, he said, "I found the students were so confused by it that I just stopped doing it because I didn't need them to be confused. I needed them to be clear, and why give them something that I can't explain any further than I had explained it? So, I just decided not to do that any more."[109] I still find the function statement useful, in the way that a mathematical proof is useful. So, writing a function statement is still part of my own work-up. (See Illustration 2.) The question, "What do you want the sermon to do?" is the one Hethcock presented to our class, which is drawn from Long's definition. Long's definition of the function statement is "a description of what the preacher hopes the sermon will create or cause to happen for the hearers."[110] When I make a function statement, it is usually not a complete sentence. Rather it completes the thought, "The function of this sermon is . . . ." Here are a couple of examples of function statements from my own work-ups, using the same pericopes for which proclamations and focus statements were given as examples:

- Function Statement for Advent 2C, Luke 3:1–18 (John appears in the wilderness.): To help us focus away from trivialities and prepare for the radical demands of the coming of Christ.
- Function Statement for 5C, Luke 5:1–11 (The unexpected catch of fish.): To recognize in the epiphanies of Christ an epiphany about who we are in relationship to Christ.

108. Hethcock, sermon, Jan. 21, 2007.
109. Interview with Hethcock, June 6, 2008.
110. Long, *The Witness of Preaching*, 86.

FINDING A CONTROLLING METAPHOR: AN OPTIONAL, OCCASIONAL ADDITION TO HETHCOCK'S PROCESS

One summer at the end of a reading course in preaching that Hethcock directed for me, I began reading and considering the work of Barbara Brown Taylor.[111] I found that Taylor's primary gift to narrative preaching lies in her rich use of metaphor. But more than her metaphorical language, I discovered in many of her sermons a "controlling metaphor" for the sermon. She shows us our "blood kinship" with Christ in the cup of communion by weaving her own story as an 8-year-old "blood sister" with the story of young adult Lebanese men whose culture included a real "blood brothers" covenant.[112] She relies on Meister Eckhart, "a medieval mystic and theologian" known for saying, "We are all meant to be mothers of God," and helps us, like Mary, become "pregnant with God" in order to assure us, "You can agree to smuggle God into the world inside your body."[113] Developing this image, this metaphor, is not an extra; it is an essential element of the sermon preparation process for Taylor. I agree that finding the metaphor is every bit as important as the focus statement. "I work," Taylor explains, "under the assumption that the development of an image is as important as the development of an idea—more important, perhaps—since there is every reason to believe that conversion is an imaginative process and not an intellectual one."[114]

As a result of this discovery, I decided to make my own optional addition to Hethcock's work-up.[115] It is the identification of a controlling metaphor. Taylor claims metaphorical preaching as being authentic because Jesus talks about God using metaphors: "Why didn't he just come right out and say what he meant? If anyone in the world were qualified to speak directly about God, surely it was Jesus, and yet he too spoke indirectly, making surprising comparisons between holy things and or-

---

111. Taylor is well-known as an Episcopal preacher, speaker, and author. She is Butman Professor of Religion at Piedmont College. Taylor has been awarded eight honorary doctor of divinity degrees, has delivered the prestigious Lyman Beecher Lectures in preaching at Yale Divinity School, and has been named by Baylor University as one of the twelve most effective preachers in the English language.

112. Taylor, "Blood Covenant," *Gospel Medicine*, 57–63.

113. Taylor, "Mothers of God," *Gospel Medicine*, 153.

114. Taylor, *Teaching Sermons*, 12.

115. In describing this idea, I make no claim to originality. Paul Scott Wilson puts forward a similar concept, which he calls "one image." See Wilson, *The Four Pages*, 50–56.

dinary things, breaking open our everyday understanding of things and inviting us to explore them all over again."[116]

Taylor's claim of this indirect method of speaking by Jesus validates a similar approach for preachers. I think that her special offering to the art of narrative preaching is the use of the metaphor to organize the core of sacred communication. "As a narrative preacher," she writes, "I am used to grabbing the metaphor implicit in an event and running with it."[117] I wonder if a metaphor is implicit in every pericope from which we preach. Should we consider identifying it along with the focus sentence and the function statement?

Perhaps a clear example of a controlling metaphor will help answer the question. Here is one from a sermon preparation for the Gospel from Proper 17B, Mark 7:1–8, 14–15, and 21–23. In this pericope, the Pharisees upbraid Jesus for his failure to have the disciples adhere to established purity codes. I decided that the human condition that could be matched up in all three locations was a set of codes that divide us. Then I decided to play with the notion of purity codes in order to allow the congregation and me to accept the fact that we, like the Pharisees, have our own purity codes. The focus sentence was, "Jesus calls us away from our particular ideas, 'correct practices,' and 'right beliefs' that divide us and back to the fundamentals of God's commandments, so that what comes out of our hearts is the kind of purity that unites us in Christ."[118] I began the sermon using the controlling metaphor, a Barbie doll birthday cake.

In a household that adheres strongly to a
  "You are what you eat" code,
    the Barbie Doll Princess Birthday Cake was *impure*.
    For one thing, she was not entirely organic.

The first-century religious leaders,
  the ones Jesus engages in this final controversy in Mark,
    would understand her impurity.

They had fenced Hebrew holiness with an elaborate set
  of purity codes regarding everything having to do with food.

---

116. Taylor, *The Seeds of Heaven*, 22.
117. Taylor, *The Luminous Web*, 16.
118. This is not the best example of a focus statement, as discussed above. It is a bit long and lacks the sharpness of a properly drawn target. For a good example, see the end of the section, "Crafting the Focus Statement," referenced by footnote 108.

As one commentator puts it,
  "They specified *what* may be eaten,
    how it is grown,
      how it is prepared,
        in *what* vessels it is served,
          when and *where* it is eaten,
            and *with whom* it may be consumed."[119]

Not unlike the specifications for the cake,
  I thought, when I read that explanation.

All the homemade cake ingredients had to be bought at the
  co-operative grocery store,
    where we could be sure what was being served
      were local interests,
        not the interests of some large national chain.

The eggs, the milk, the unbleached flour, even the powdered sugar,
  all had to be grown organically.
    Indeed, the powdered sugar wore a label announcing
      that it was the only organic powdered sugar
        manufactured in the United States!

However, two things made Barbie impure.
  One was the Crisco.
    In case you have not looked, let me assure you,
      there is *no such thing* as organic Crisco.

But decorator icing,
  the kind that can be shoved down into a tube
    and squeezed out through a tip
      to give it that star-burst shape,
        that kind of icing calls for Crisco,
          defiling though it may be.

---

119. Neyrey, "A Symbolic Approach to Mark 7," 3.3, available at www.nd.edu/~jneyrey1/symbolic.html. Emphasis in the original.

The blonde Barbie presented other problems.
    She towered 12 inches above the 12-inch-round bottom layer,
        surrounded by 8 upended quarters of the two 9-inch rounds,
            which gave her an impressive skirt.
                But Barbie, built as she was, like all Barbies,
                    was a politically incorrect doll
                        for a Princess birthday cake.

Indeed, for her to be acceptable,
    after she had been fished out of her attic hiding place,
        she had to be surrounded by green and yellow icing stars
            so as to "un-flatter" her figure.
                Even this was not completely redeeming
                    since the bathing suit bodice still showed,
                    and the powdered sugar icing
                        was defiled with un-organic Crisco.

Yet, there she stood in violation of our purity codes,
    ready to preside,
        one hand uplifted in a princess wave.

Illustration 3. A Controlling Metaphor

Metaphors in preaching have real staying power, which is probably why I remember a sermon by a preacher named Paul Bailey in the late 1990s. He was preaching on the rich young man story (Mark 10:17–22), which ends with Jesus telling the young man to go sell his belongings and give to the poor. Bailey told of a new puppy with a special toy. During the sermon he kept returning to the dog and its changing relationship with that toy. The toy started out as an aid to playing with Bailey, but by the time the sermon ended, the old dog was standing over the toy, snarling at anyone who approached and threatened to remove it. I cannot hear that Gospel without seeing the old dog protecting his possession in the way we protect ours. Bailey's metaphor changed the way I hear that Gospel. Now, instead of hearing an admonition I'm unlikely to take seriously (sell all you own and give it to the poor), I hear a call to examine the role my possessions play in the relationships to which God calls me, including relationships with the poor.

Now that we have completed the process from exegesis to focus statement and have explained the optional steps of a function statement and a controlling metaphor, it is time to craft the sermon itself. As our first task in chapter 3, we will stop to ask how all this fits into Hethcock's theology of preaching.

3

Stopping to Consider
Hethcock's Theology of Preaching

One lovely Sewanee evening at a reception, I stood on a wide front porch chatting with a man a half generation older than I. He knew I was a priest in the Episcopal Church. What do you talk about with a priest at a reception? The church, of course. Somehow he wandered off into the topic of the civil rights movement and how, in the 1960s, he was attending a large Protestant church that became infected by the White Citizens' Council. The Council members managed to intimidate some of the church leadership but not the chief pastor of the church. As groups of African Americans began appearing at the doors of "all white" congregations, the chief pastor let the White Citizens' Council know that all God's children were welcome in that church.

One Sunday morning some African-American worshipers did appear. The White Citizens' Council members rose and began roughly ushering the African Americans out of the church. But the chief pastor, who was then in the pulpit, stopped mid-sentence. He announced, "I am resigning this pulpit. Right Now." And he did. He stopped preaching, resigned, moved to another state to live with his son, and never pastored a church again. The associate pastor tried to stick it out for awhile. Eventually, the associate pastor had to explain to the leaders that even though he might be able to withstand the telephone threats, he had a family and children. So, he also left.

Then my reception friend said they brought in "scab" preachers, the ones who would tell three or four jokes every sermon and never say anything of substance. My mind went to a plastic frame on the wall in my study that has been in place since I finished seminary. It holds 2 Timothy 4:2–5, typed out in Gothic script on nice ecru stationery, a gift from Bill Hethcock to each of his preaching students at the end of our middle year of seminary. "For the time is coming," says the pastoral letter, "when

Stopping to Consider Hethcock's Theology of Preaching 57

people will not put up with sound doctrine, but having itching ears they will accumulate for themselves teachers to suit their own desires, and will turn away from listening to the truth and wander away to myths."[1] I was suddenly aware of what "itching ears" could mean, of what it was like to choose scab preachers "to suit their own likings." At the same time, I was aware that my reception friend knew exactly what those scab preachers were doing, had no respect for them, did not need and could not use their sermons.

It is not likely that we will face the scab preacher epitaph. And it is unlikely we will be called to lay ourselves on the line in quite the same way clergy were called upon during the civil rights movement. In ten years of serving as a priest, the strongest instances of opposition I have faced were a couple of occasions when someone walked out in the middle of a sermon. Yet it is clear that congregations today also need something that congregations in the 1960s needed. They need the confrontation of God's grace.

Hethcock calls it "supportive confrontation," the kind that leads to transformation. "Transformation, if it is well done," says Hethcock, "comes as 'good news.' Supportive confrontation means that the bad news, if you want to call it that, where we fall short or we aren't what we are meant to be, is preached in such a way that it becomes good news."[2] Supportive confrontation that leads to transformation grows out of the central message of preaching when individuals understand and accept God's involvement in their lives. What is the main thing, the central message that needs to be heard in preaching? Hethcock answers, "That God is closer, nearer, more attentive, and [more] involved in our lives than we are aware. A sermon that does not allow us to be aware of and experience that again is probably less effective than it ought to be."[3] What is it we really want to say about what this God is doing with us, this God who is closer, nearer, and more attentive than we imagine? How is this God going to use what the preacher says to interact with the people in the pew? These questions go to the theology of preaching.

So far, our discussion in this book has centered more on matters of communication than on matters concerning the theology of preaching. It is apparent that theology underlies Hethcock's careful approach

1. 2 Tim 4:3–4.
2. Interview with Hethcock, May 30, 2008.
3. Interview with Hethcock, May 30, 2008.

in preparing to preach, but now we need to stop and linger with that theology a bit. Perhaps the best resource is an essay Hethcock wrote for a Festschrift honoring church historian Donald S. Armentrout in 2003.[4] The substance of this essay had been Hethcock's final lecture for senior seminarians. A former student, Thomas Macfie, then rector of Otey Memorial Parish in Sewanee (and now chaplain of All Saints' Chapel at the University of the South), suggested that Hethcock write up the lecture for publication.[5]

In the essay, Hethcock posits that "sermons may still lack the serious depth that would better serve congregations"; that "preachers settle in their sermons for surface interpretation that falls short of deeper and more challenging biblical messages present in the readings"; that the gospel can be "trivialized" by this kind of preaching; and, finally, that the congregation has been shortchanged by a failure "to reveal the more confrontational biblical challenge."[6]

There is a cliché that the preacher is called upon to "comfort the afflicted and afflict the comfortable." At the beginning of his essay, "'Crossing the River:' Proclaiming Deeper Truth from the Pulpit," Hethcock recognizes these seemingly contradictory roles in preaching. He says, "When we preach, our safe assumption is that the people in the congregation need to be comforted. They need to be loved. Their self-esteem needs to be reinforced. Their lives need to become meaningful for them." Because this need for comfort is a universal condition for time-bound creatures, "whether they have not yet survived the difficulties of yesterday or whether they are struggling with relentless anxiety over tomorrow," we can be sure that those in our congregations "feel a measure of discomfort—dread, if you please—about what is going on for them in their lives."[7] In various ways, we are all afflicted and need, whether we realize it or not, for God to comfort us.

---

4. Hethcock, "'Crossing the River,'" 145–170. This is the essay Hethcock wrote in honor of Donald S. Armentrout, his colleague at the SofT. "Crossing the River" refers to a significant point in Urban T. Holmes, III's book, *A Priest in Community*. The essay's subtitle, "Proclaiming Deeper Truth from the Pulpit," more accurately describes Hethcock's essay. The essays submitted for this event were collected in a volume edited by Ralph K. Hawkins.

5. Interview with Hethcock, June 4, 2008.

6. Hethcock, "'Crossing the River,'" 146.

7. Hethcock, "'Crossing the River,'" 148.

Stopping to Consider Hethcock's Theology of Preaching

Hethcock acknowledges that the overall biblical message is full of comfort that needs to be spoken from the pulpit and heard by congregations. However, he cautions preachers about the possibility of temporary comfort. After some men and women have been "encouraged and strengthened," he says, . . . "[t]hey will leave the church refreshed and ready to move on, whether in strength or in difficulty, *until their dark feelings return to cast shadows once again on their temporary successes*."[8] Hethcock then shows the preacher the place where there is a fusion between comforting the afflicted and afflicting the comfortable with a God who is nearer to us than we imagined. He writes,

> The point is that such "repair and maintenance," [that is, temporary encouragement and strengthening] invaluable though it may be in the short run, is nonetheless in the long run no substitute for the crucial change that a listener needs to make, the serious confrontation with the self, as well as with the world, with an eye to discovering often painful truths that, when faced with courage, become the friends needed for new life in the world and provide a richer understanding of God. . . . Their preaching requires a goal that goes deeper than strength and comfort, one that moves us toward and encourages change.[9]

For preachers, practicing the concept of "supportive confrontation" is an essential element of Hethcock's theology. Supportive confrontation is that place where the congregation can be challenged or confronted (or afflicted as in the cliché) by a more-attentive-than-expected God, and because of that confrontation they will be supported in the kind of change that brings real and lasting comfort. Supportive confrontation is the place where preaching the bad news becomes the vehicle though which the good news can be heard. As preachers, we need to discover that place and create a climate of trust and openness, so that our interpretations of scripture can be explored honestly and in depth. If we can do this, we will not reach the point of desperation, where our integrity demands resignation and the scab preachers begin taking over.

Hethcock explains,

> When we really get down to what Jesus is saying, it is confrontational and demanding, and we are brought up under judgment. And that is bad news. But in a sense the judgment is good news

---

8. Hethcock, "'Crossing the River,'" 148 (emphasis in original).
9. Hethcock, "'Crossing the River,'" 148–49.

because we are never going to grow unless we recognize that we are being judged and what the judgment says. And what we know about Jesus is that what he says he says out of his compassion for us, so that even his judgment is a loving act. And it is comforting in the sense of "f-o-r-t," which is strengthening. So, we should come away from the sermon having been confronted with where we are at fault or where we are weak and our need to change and grow, but strengthened, not beaten down, but ready and aware to do it.[10]

Regarding this confrontation, Hethcock says, "That needs to be given without pulling the rug out from under Jesus, with no effort to water it [Jesus' message] down in any kind of way. That is the blatant demand of the Gospel and of the Gospel of Jesus Christ. However, people need not be left there. They need to know that they are enabled by the presence of Christ within them, by the presence of the Spirit, to accomplish the good that the Gospel demands."[11]

How, then, does the preacher supportively confront the people in the pews? Hethcock answers,

> In the proclamation, we are going to come up with the here and now human condition, and it is going to be in touch with the scripture [the exegesis]. And if you want to call it [the human condition] bad news, you can. It is not really bad news. If the sermon ended there, we would be out on a limb, having been confronted but not helped. The sermon must include for the listener [the assurance] that we can do what the scripture has called for. We are enabled by the grace of God and by the work of the Spirit to grow and become better. So the judgment of the scripture does not bring us to hopelessness unless the preacher quits too early. It brings us to hope and to joy in growth.[12]

For the preacher to do all of this for the listeners, the preacher must first confront him/herself with the bad or painful news in the text. Hethcock writes, "The new experience starts with the preacher.... After we discover the good news that helps us to feel good and to approach a new week with renewed optimism, there is still more. What is that other good news that calls our status quo into question and demands of us a

---

10. Interview with Hethcock, June 4, 2008.
11. Interview with Hethcock, June 4, 2008.
12. Interview with Hethcock, June 4, 2008.

hard look at who we are and whether we are permitted in the will of God to continue to be that person alone?"[13]

Referring to the work of John A. T. Robinson and Frederick Buechner, Hethcock claims this kind of good news must touch down into our center or inner selves. Only after the preacher has engaged with the text at that deep level of inner self can the preacher invite the congregation to join in. Hethcock says the "best model we have for preaching that consistently touches" this inner self/this center comes from the African-American experience. Using the work of William Augustus Jones, Jr., and Henry H. Mitchell, Hethcock presents traditional black preaching as having "a telling relevance to the kind of dramatic relationship to today's human need required in all our pulpits."[14] To me this is true because in traditional black preaching, the "bad" news is so clearly identified and brought into the experience of the congregation that listeners are emotionally open to the "good" news, ready for their inner selves to be touched deep down and transformed. Hethcock elucidates this model by quoting Jones: "The historic reality of existential dehumanization over against the recognition of essential dignity demands a word from the Lord. And that word of hope, deliverance, and liberation has reverberated in black churches across America all along the pathway of our pilgrimage."[15]

In other words, the congregation is more likely to be transformed by the good news that might come from a particular text after the individuals in the congregation have experienced the bad news of dehumanization and then are reminded that their essential human dignity is grounded in God—through whom hope, deliverance, and liberation come. Dehumanization or being deprived of positive human qualities is not restricted to being discriminated against because of one's race, religion, gender, or tribe. It happens whenever one person treats another as an object or when one group demonizes another group as its enemy.

If we look back to chapter 2, we can begin to understand the necessity of locating a human condition that has legs in, that touches down into the scripture, into the community for which the scripture was first written, into the preacher's experience, and then into the congregation for which the sermon will be preached. It is that specific piece of bad news the preacher and congregation must first experience before any specific piece of the good news can be brought to bear.

13. Hethcock, "'Crossing the River,'" 148–49.
14. Hethcock, "'Crossing the River,'" 155.
15. Jones, "Introduction," 5, quoted in Hethcock, "'Crossing the River,'" 153.

In order to mine further the kind of good news that speaks to our human condition, Hethcock turns to the work of Urban T. Holmes III, who was dean of the School of Theology when Hethcock arrived to teach there in 1979. They had met as undergraduates at the University of North Carolina in the 1950s, and both men had been drawn to the work of Carl Jung. As he renewed his friendship with Holmes, Hethcock says, "I began to discover how much of the thinking I had done in a rudimentary sense he had taken far beyond that. We were at the same place on many things." Holmes' most well-known work is *A Priest in Community: Exploring the Roots of Ministry*.[16] In that book, Holmes develops a metaphor Hethcock refers to as "a landscape of reality." After researching Jung's work and calling friends of Holmes after his death,[17] Hethcock concluded that Holmes' metaphor was Jungian but not one specifically attributable to Jung. "I could never find the origin of the story on the landscape of reality," says Hethcock. "I don't know whether it is his or whether it is adapted from something else."[18]

In "'Crossing the River': Proclaiming Deeper Truth from the Pulpit," Hethcock explores Holmes' extended landscape of reality metaphor, which involves a river banked on one side by a landscape of civilized order (active/analytical/rational mode) and on the other side by a landscape of wilderness (receptive/holistic/intuitive mode) over which the preacher is required to stand, one foot on each bank of the river.[19] Hethcock describes what is required of the preacher:

> So standing [over the river], they [preachers] must use informed wisdom to discern the gospel truth, and with Spirit-strengthened will to give us sermons that guide us into visits to the receptive mode of consciousness.
>
> Alas, many preach without even having made the journey themselves, so they are hardly in a position to encourage others to do so. The ordered, rational, logical sermon, devised solely on this structured side of the river where we live, is tragically limited, as is the shallow religious experience with which it must make do.[20]

16. Holmes, *A Priest in Community*.

17. Hethcock arrived at the SofT in August 1979, and Holmes died "on the Feast of the Transfiguration [August 6] 1980." Interview with Hethcock, June 4, 2008.

18. Interview with Hethcock, June 4, 2008.

19. Hethcock, "'Crossing the River,'" 155–57.

20. Hethcock, "'Crossing the River,'" 157.

Hethcock wants the preacher to make that journey into the receptive mode, where "ambiguity is not only widely prevalent, . . . [but] welcomed," where the Eucharist is celebrated as mystery, not for understanding, where the church's doctrines become "tools for thinking, wondering and risky decision-making," but where faith is received as divine gift through our own vulnerability, where doubt points out limitations and calls us to prayer, where the priest discovers "how to utter words that shake loose our acquired and tutored limitations."[21]

He illustrates by reference to an Easter 1 sermon, preached on John 20:19–31, when the risen Christ encounters the incredulous disciple, Thomas. "Thomas' coming to believe is an effort to cross the river because it says there is a different kind of believing than the cognitive believing. To touch and feel is a different kind of believing. And, it is a believing with the heart."[22]

How do we get there, across the river into the receptive mode where all this can happen? Hethcock admits no formula, "no 'how-to' instructions for such a quest," and instead offers "ruminations" on three biblical themes as a guide. They are the "in Christ" theme from the Pauline correspondence, the "abide" theme from the Johannine literature, and the "kingdom" language of the Synoptic Gospels.[23] In the Episcopal Church, unless the preacher has decided to focus on a reading from the Hebrew scripture, non-Pauline correspondence, or the Apocrypha, one of these overarching themes is likely to be at play. The rest of Hethcock's essay is spent exploring these themes. A summary here would not do his exploration justice; readers will be best served by a review of the article. However, to offer insights into the essay's key concepts, a few quotations follow.

- As a result of being "in Christ," we view ourselves and one another differently: "One who is 'in Christ' is not only seen from a different point of view but also looks at others with an eye to the inner person rather than the outer visible person."[24]
- The "abide" language in the Johannine literature points to a particularly strong kind of intimacy: "We can legitimately infer a genuine intimacy in Jesus' use of 'abide.' We are called on to keep Jesus' commandments, the principal one of which is to love, and

21. Hethcock, "'Crossing the River,'" 158.
22. Interview with Hethcock, June 4, 2008.
23. Hethcock, "'Crossing the River,'" 158–168.
24. Hethcock, "'Crossing the River,'" 160.

by doing so to abide in his love, just as Jesus abides in the Father's love. The same kind of intimacy in the relationship between the Father and the Son is available to each of us as we approach a relationship with Jesus. [Jesus] speaks of . . . their [the disciples'] continuing in a relationship that demonstrates ongoing mutual loyalty and commitment."[25]

- Finally, the 'kingdom' language of the Synoptic Gospels cannot be understood absent self-surrender and a necessarily metaphorical approach to the meaning of the cross: "The parables [about the kingdom] continue to be hidden and puzzling for as long as we resist Jesus' call. Only when we become his disciples does the mystery of the kingdom unfold. In my opinion, at the heart of the ethic of the breaking-in kingdom lie the verses that refer to the self-surrender required of those who desire to become Jesus' followers."[26] ". . . [L]osing one's life and taking up one's cross . . . lie at the heart of his kingdom ethic."[27] ". . . This saying [about the cross] must remain metaphorical for its meaning to retain its power; otherwise you and I might excuse ourselves from it since there appears to be no [literal] cross in our future."[28] "When we take up our cross, we will, like Jesus, place ourselves over against the demands of the culture in order to speak and live the gospel Jesus is delivering to us."[29]

In some manner, the good news that is to be found by being "in Christ," by "abiding" with God, or by coming into the "kingdom of God"[30] or "kingdom of heaven"[31] impacts our overarching human condition, which Hethcock describes in this way: "The human predicament is that our primary enterprise in life is grasping all that we can for ourselves, making ourselves the center of our own universe. This is the means of

---

25. Hethcock, "'Crossing the River,'" 163–64.
26. Hethcock, "'Crossing the River,'" 165.
27. Hethcock, "'Crossing the River,'" 166.
28. Hethcock, "'Crossing the River,'" 166.
29. Hethcock, "'Crossing the River,'" 167.
30. For a full treatment of "kingdom of God," see Hethcock, "Preaching the Kingdom of God," 163–185.
31. The Matthean term that Hethcock describes as a "Jewish reverential circumlocution" for "kingdom of God." See Hethcock's "Exegesis for Proper 6, Year A," 27.

gaining life, of saving life, in the world. Living in this manner will leave us, Jesus is saying, with no life at all."[32]

Here, then, is the connection between the process of preparing the sermon and Hethcock's theology of preaching. There is a necessary connection between the process and the theology, he says, "because you could use the process in such a way that you only skim the surface if in step one you don't really investigate what the scripture may be saying and meaning; then steps two and three need not go very deep. But if you took seriously the need to say from the pulpit the deepest, perhaps even the most difficult and challenging dimension of the reading at hand, if you do that, that is what I am talking about that would be the point at which it [the process] would connect with the [theological discussion in the] article."[33]

Hethcock's theology of preaching begins, then, with the recognition that God is nearer and more involved in our lives than we might imagine and calls upon the preacher to do more in a sermon than provide temporary comfort. His theology calls upon the preacher to go deeply into the text for the sermon and find the place where the news of a specific human condition is touched by the transforming good news of God's grace, bring it out, and offer it up in a way that it can be heard and received by the congregation. In the Pauline literature, the preacher looks for that good news "in Christ." In the Johannine literature, the preacher looks for it in Jesus' love, the place where we are being called to "abide." In the Synoptics, the preacher looks for the good news as part of the "kingdom" into which Christ is calling us. When a congregation is both confronted and comforted with the depth of the good news, the preacher assists in unleashing God's transforming grace. When this level of preaching occurs, it is hoped that most people in the congregation will not develop "itching ears" for the kind of scab preaching that turns them "away from listening to the truth."[34] Instead, the hope is that listeners will choose to be transformed through Christ's love and God's grace into living more closely to the Gospel.

---

32. Hethcock, "'Crossing the River,'" 168.
33. Interview with Hethcock, June 4, 2008.
34. See 2 Tim 4:3–4.

4

Making Your Way into the Written Sermon Script

Hethcock's sixth lecture for the fall 2004 homiletics course at Virginia Theological Seminary is about preaching using the homiletical method of Eugene Lowry. Hethcock recommends Lowry's sense of plot and story to his class. He tells them, "If I, we, could learn to use Lowry's method well, we would discover that the congregation authenticates the sermon by their experience[s] as they listen, and a real sermon has 'happened.'" Then, referencing his own teaching, he compares Lowry's method to his. He tells the class that his method will take them through the study and up to the focus sentence and that Lowry's method "is a guide to the crafting of the sermon from the focus sentence on to its delivery in the pulpit."[1]

In assigning one of Lowry's books[2] to his students, Hethcock says, "The reader is not likely to preach precisely as Lowry recommends; rather, each of us uses this kind of text to discover our own best method of crafting and preaching a sermon."[3] Hethcock uses Lowry's work to promote the idea that a sermon should have the qualities of a story. "I want to say the sermon is not actually a story," Hethcock explains, "but it is like a story." By this he means that the sermon will have a plot that moves toward proclamation. To explain further, Hethcock quotes Lowry: "I see every sermon as an event-in-time, which . . . moves from opening disequilibrium through escalation of conflict to surprising reversal to closing denouement (in which the table of life gets set for us in a new way by the gospel)."[4]

---

1. Unpublished lecture notes, VTS, lecture 6, 2.
2. Lowry, *The Homiletical Plot*.
3. Unpublished syllabus, VTS, 2.
4. Lowry, *How to Preach*, 25, quoted in unpublished lecture notes, VTS, lecture 5, 2.

Lowry recommends five parts for a narrative sermon, which Hethcock summarizes and teaches to his students using the following list: "1) upsetting the equilibrium (oops), 2) analyzing the discrepancy (ugh), 3) disclosing the clue to resolution (aha), 4) experiencing the gospel (whee), and 5) anticipating the consequences (yeah)."[5] For our purposes, we will stay with the spirit of Lowry's technique without progressing through each part. The quote above points to a more fluid and general understanding of narrative movement from opening disequilibrium to conflict ("trouble" is Lowry's word) to reversal to denouement (or "crank-down" in Hethcock's terminology).

The sermon, Hethcock suggests, is not like a bunch of grapes that are connected to each other in some loose way. Rather, it is like a road, linear in nature, moving toward its proclamation. Hethcock tells his students:

> One of the ways Lowry has described the movement within the sermon is that it does not follow the pattern of "this *and* this *and* this *and* this *and* this." Instead, the pattern it follows is "this *then* this *then* this *then* this *then* this." The difference is that "this *and* this *and* this" is a collection of ideas that do not necessarily follow one another. However, "this *then* this *then* this" is a progression of ideas each one of which depends upon the idea that precedes it and leads to another, the next, idea. The listeners are waiting to hear what will come next. . . . It is the *progression of ideas* from the beginning along a *plot line* that makes the sermon like a short story, that is, that makes the sermon a *narrative sermon*.[6]

However, Hethcock wants students to distinguish between a "story sermon," one that weaves exegesis, human condition, and proclamation into an actual story the preacher is telling, and a "narrative sermon," one that moves along a plot line. A story sermon would be a subcategory of a narrative sermon. A narrative sermon, however, need not actually tell a story. Using the classic television situation comedy to illustrate, Hethcock maintains that the narrative sermon begins when things are "normal, peaceful, as expected" and moves to "conflict, trouble, upset of the equilibrium" as "one thing leads to another," to a point of "climax"

---

5. Unpublished lecture notes, SofT, hours 7–8, 6. These are also included in handout no. 7, VTS, "Your Itch and Scratch Workbook," along with three of Hethcock's sermons in which he tracks Lowry's five steps. See Lowry, *The Homiletical Plot*, 26, for steps 28–87 and for analysis.

6. Unpublished lecture notes, VTS, lecture 5, 4.

or what Lowry calls "reversal," and then into "crank-down" or "denouement" right after the final commercial.[7]

I admit to some difficulty understanding how such a narrative movement could take place without being an actual "story," so one of Hethcock's sermons is helpful to me as an illustration. The one I have chosen was preached at Bruton Parish in Williamsburg, Virginia, on January 16, 2000, the second Sunday after Epiphany.[8] The controlling text is John 1:43–51. In this gospel reading, Andrew, Peter, and Philip from Bethsaida are already following Jesus when Philip finds Nathanael in Galilee and tells him about Jesus. Nathanael, who first asks incredulously, "Can anything good come out of Nazareth?" ends up proclaiming directly to Jesus, "Rabbi, you are the Son of God! You are the King of Israel!"

In the gospel reading, just after Jesus has told Nathanael, "Very truly, I tell you, you will see heaven opened and the angels of God ascending and descending upon the Son of Man," members of the congregation at Bruton settle into their box seats, and Hethcock begins.

GETTING STARTED

Before I relate his sermon, let's think about some good ways to get started. When I was in elementary school and we were just learning to give speeches, my father told me a speech had three parts: Tell them what you are going to tell them. Tell them. Tell them what you have told them. Though a surprising number of preachers may still be following my father's advice, this is *not* what Hethcock recommends. Instead, Hethcock tells his students that no introduction of a sermon is necessary. When the congregation sits and looks up at the preacher, the preacher has the attention of those in the nave. It is up to the preacher to keep that attention or lose it. Liturgically, no prayer, no hymn, no invocation of the Trinity should interrupt the flow of the service at this point.[9] The Gospel has been proclaimed; we are at the apex of the service of the word. The transition from Gospel to sermon is intended to be seamless. The thing to do is start.

---

7. Unpublished lecture notes, VTS, lecture 5, 4–5.

8. This sermon is one of nineteen sermons Bruton Parish printed in a booklet honoring Hethcock's preaching during the six months he served as interim associate rector at the historic parish, beginning in October 1999. Hethcock, *Sermons Preached*.

9. Unpublished handout, VTS, "Invocations and 'Amens.'"

I have found that there are three good places to start. One is inside the controlling pericope for the sermon. A second is inside the human condition that the preacher has matched up in three places—by focusing there and then in the pericope, there and then in the early Christian community, or here and now in the lives of the congregation. A third possibility is inside the controlling metaphor if the preacher has chosen one to facilitate the proclamation. Hethcock begins this particular sermon inside the human condition here and now.

The congregation is seated. They look up to the pulpit. In the gospel lesson, Jesus has just finished talking about angels ascending and descending. Hethcock says, "I was listening to public radio when I heard about a scientist who is publishing a unique paper. He is revealing his discovery that when iguanas are short of food their bodies shrink."[10] Is this sermon designed to be heard? Are you listening? What are you thinking? Well, I don't know what you are thinking, but I will tell you what I am thinking. I am wondering what in the world iguanas have to do with angels! Was there an iguana under that fig tree with Nathanael? Where in the world is this man going with this sermon? Not sure. He has not lost my attention—not yet.

It is important to realize that iguanas cannot be a gimmick. I am willing to continue listening because over time Hethcock has taught me that nothing he says from the pulpit is intended to be discarded. I trust that somehow this narrative about iguanas has to do with what he wants to proclaim about the interaction we have just heard between Jesus and Nathanael. If iguanas (or any other novel illustrations) are a gimmick, the preacher may get away with it once or twice, but soon enough the congregation will catch on and check out so as not to be cheated.

Soon we learn that Hethcock is talking about *assumptions*. Scientists now know that starved iguanas actually shrink in size, their bones shrink, and they get shorter. Even though this was going on right before the eyes of the scientists, they assumed it could not be so. They assumed they were getting the iguanas confused or that there was some other explanation for the apparent change in the iguanas' size. He tells us, "All scientists observing the shrinking of iguanas up to now have denied their observed data until this one scientist overcame his assumption and trusted what he saw to be true."[11] Here is an excellent example of the

---

10. Hethcock, *Sermons Preached*, 62.
11. Hethcock, *Sermons Preached*, 62.

human condition. We make assumptions about what is truth, and we become so attached to our assumptions that we are unable to grasp new truth. Hethcock says, "This radio report explains that failure to make this discovery about the shrinking iguanas earlier happened because of the mistaken assumption by the scientists."[12]

Without further comment, Hethcock continues. "Philip has just met Jesus. . . ." Note what he does not say. He does not say, "Now let us return to our gospel lesson this morning." The congregation has just heard the gospel lesson and can be trusted to return there immediately when it is mentioned, notwithstanding the insertion of iguanas.[13]

FROM LOWRY: THIS *THEN* THIS, *THEN* THIS, *THEN* THIS

Having returned to the biblical story, Hethcock lays out the status quo or equilibrium. Nathanael, it turns out, has something in common with those iguana-studying scientists; he is an authority. Hethcock knows this from his exegetical work-up. He is not going to take the congregation into the library and pull some commentary off the shelf. A sermon is not a research paper. "The fig tree tells us something about Nathanael. A rabbi who was a serious scholar traditionally sat under a fig tree. Nathanael is a learned authority. He knows his facts. He knows how the Messiah, the Christ, is foretold to appear. Based on all the information Nathanael has learned through his years as a rabbinical scholar, the Messiah will never come from Nazareth in Galilee. Therefore, Nathanael *assumes* that this Jesus whom Philip has met cannot be the Christ."[14] A plot line is developing in which the identified human condition represents the equilibrium, or status quo, that will be impacted by the gospel proclamation. We are moving into disequilibrium.

We might be ready to say, "I see. This is about making assumptions." Such a statement would be a conclusion. As Hethcock has done

---

12. Hethcock, *Sermons Preached*, 62.

13. There is a method of intertwining two stories, one from the biblical pericope and the other a contemporary story of the preacher's choice, a technique Hethcock attributes to a friend of his, homilist Charles Rice. Hethcock credits Rice with the term "layering" for this process. In one article, though not speaking exclusively or specifically about layering, Rice proposes that the "preacher *moves* constantly back and forth between the world of the biblical story and the particular time, place, and people with whom he or she has to do, including oneself." Rice, "Shaping Sermons," 104.

14. Hethcock, *Sermons Preached*, 63 (italics added).

the inductive work and brought us along, he is ready now to say that explicitly. "The scientists who failed to notice the phenomenon of shrinking iguanas were misguided by their mistaken assumptions. Nathanael's failure to recognize Philip's truth about Jesus Christ is caused by his own misguided assumptions. He assumes that nothing good can come out of Nazareth."[15] Again, it is unnecessary to cue the congregation to return to iguanas and then back to Nathanael because the plot line is moving along a description of the human condition. The equilibrium is about to be disturbed.

This description of the human condition (the willingness to make mistaken assumptions), *then* this further elaboration of that condition (Nathanael's assumption that this cannot be Jesus because nothing good comes from Nazareth) continue the sermon. We learn that Nathanael is highly regarded; that he received rabbinical training; and that he is bright, diligent, well meaning, and faithful. Although Hethcock does not say so directly, Nathanel just might be like us; therefore, we might share his human condition. "Nathanel thinks he knows all he needs to know, but right now he can't see beyond the shade of his fig tree."[16] Indeed, ". . . he is allowing himself to be stuck where he is with whatever assumption he already has."[17]

We do not have to identify with Nathanel or these iguana scientists. Nothing Hethcock has said requires that, but he has opened the possibility. This opening of the possibility that we might identify with the human condition is *then* followed by this: the broadening and deepening of the human condition among those with whom we probably will identify. Who are they? They are the devout religious people of Jesus' time who happen to be the Pharisees, the Jewish leaders, and the Levites. In order for Hethcock to get us to identify with them, he first has to tell us who they are. Pharisees have a bum rap among us Christians because they are so, well, pharisaic, or so hypocritical, we think. Hethcock tells us, "Those people, those Pharisees and Jewish leaders and Levites and others from Jerusalem, aren't hypocritical or irreligious or unduly self-serving or stubborn—not at first. Actually, they are dedicated, sincere, diligent, religious, devout persons. Jesus' adversaries are people who worship."[18]

15. Hethcock, *Sermons Preached*, 63.
16. Hethcock, *Sermons Preached*, 64.
17. Hethcock, *Sermons Preached*, 64.
18. Hethcock, *Sermons Preached*, 64.

What are we doing here, sitting in the pews at Bruton parish listening to this sermon? Are we being hypocritical or irreligious or self-serving? No, we are worshipping.

This *then* is followed by this observation. "But the religious leaders who meet Jesus have one fatal flaw."[19] Their fatal flaw: "*They have learned their lessons so well that when truth comes right at them, right in front of them, they cannot recognize it, because that truth does not come the way they assume it should.*"[20] That fatal flaw leads Nathanael to conclude, "No, Philip. This Jesus is from Nazareth. He couldn't be the Christ."[21]

On a plot line Hethcock has opened with the status quo, he has moved us into some disequilibrium, and he has deepened the disequilibrium in the then and there of the gospel text. He has deepened it to the point of anticipated conflict. This *then* is followed by a set of descriptions of conflict resulting from strongly held assumptions, the kind of conflict that comes closer to the here and now human condition in the lives of the congregation.

"I remember going in the mid-1960s with our bishop to a meeting at a large downtown parish in the Diocese of North Carolina," Hethcock says, immediately after Nathanael's pronouncement that Jesus could not be the Christ. At the meeting, they met "good people." Hethcock observed that "any priest would be glad and proud to be their rector."[22] Obviously, they are like us, but they also share the fatal flaw. He said that they had learned from their own parish that the diocesan conference center should not be operating programs for black and white people together. "It was," says Hethcock, "their misunderstanding of the gospel, their untested assumption that prevented them from seeing their error right there in front of them."[23] This *then* is followed by *this*, a further elaboration and investigation of the type of conflict that deepens as assumptions harden. Good people, "not uninformed or spiritually lazy," conclude that women may not be priests. "Many of them have simply learned an ancient lesson so well that they cannot consider anything

---

19. Hethcock, *Sermons Preached*, 65.
20. Hethcock, *Sermons Preached*, 65 (emphasis in original).
21. Hethcock, *Sermons Preached*, 65.
22. Hethcock, *Sermons Preached*, 65–66.
23. Hethcock, *Sermons Preached*, 66.

new. Their assumption is that there is something wrong about the ordination of women, and they don't want to look at the subject again."[24]

Sitting in the pews at Bruton, we might be wondering if this could still be going on today. Could good people still be making assumptions and be unable to look at a subject again or recognize the truth right in front of them? Is it possible that we are among those good people? Hethcock tells us this human condition is in the current climate and that it invades even our seminary education. From eighteen years of teaching experience, he tells us that some students arrive warned by "friends in their churches at home not to investigate any new ideas or teaching about theology or the Bible or ethics or Christian Education."[25] The seminary faculty has to "convince some students that it is safe to think." They have to tell students, "It is not only o.k. to question our assumptions, but it is also appropriate to challenge them and test them rigorously if we are to be spiritually alive with an able conscience and an open will."[26]

As we listen to this sermon, we are opening to the possibility of testing our assumptions and facing the truth when Hethcock says, "The toughest issue facing the Episcopal Church today regards our thinking about human sexuality."[27] We have moved from equilibrium, to disequilibrium, to conflict, to being open to the possibility of reversal, but now the assumption Hethcock will propose we test is not an historic assumption already proved to be false. It is an assumption we are currently making, the validity of which is in the process of being tested. Now we are in a position for the gospel proclamation to happen in our own lives, not just in a position to learn about how the gospel proclamation happened in the scripture or happened at some earlier point in history. Hethcock has come this far just to make us vulnerable to the proclamation. Regarding our thinking about human sexuality, Hethcock says, "In a sensible and sensitive discussion, the kind already going on in these years of study, people can make themselves willing to examine their assumptions. A standoff is not helpful. We need to be strongly invited and urged to suspend our assumptions long enough to look at the subject afresh, openly,

---

24. Hethcock, *Sermons Preached*, 66.
25. Hethcock, *Sermons Preached*, 66.
26. Hethcock, *Sermons Preached*, 66.
27. Hethcock, *Sermons Preached*, 67.

compassionately, and wisely."[28] We are now open to that possibility when Hethcock moves to the gospel proclamation.

He begins, "Joseph Fletcher, one time noted ethicist and professor of ethics, told of an experience he once had." Following Lowry's pattern of this *then* this, Hethcock continues to tell of Fletcher's experience with a St. Louis taxi driver. "The taxi driver told Fletcher about the strong allegiance of his family to one political party and how that tradition had been handed down to him. 'Well,' said Fletcher, 'you'll be voting for your party's candidate this year, won't you?' 'On no, not this year,' said the cab driver. 'There comes a time,' he said, 'when you have to give up what you believe in order to do what's right.'"[29] There it is. From iguanas to Nathanael and then vice versa, then from commitment to racial segregation, to commitment to male-only clergy, to assumptions of those being trained for the ministry, then to our own assumptions in current conflicts around matters of human sexuality, and finally, when we are sufficiently open to it—*then* there it is, the proclamation, in what may well be this sermon's focus sentence from the mouth of a taxi driver: "There comes a time when you have to give up what you believe in order to do what's right." As Lowry would say it, we are at the plot point of reversal.

"As it develops, there under the fig tree, Nathanael is willing to open up a little after all,"[30] Hethcock continues, immediately after revealing the taxi driver's proclamation. Hethcock next authenticates our experience of the gospel proclamation with the Gospel itself. He says that Nathanael, by giving up "what he believes in order to do what is right," is able to respond "with a statement of believing beyond that of any other witness the Gospel of John has named so far" when Nathanael says, "'Rabbi, you are the Son of God! You are the King of Israel!'"[31] We are now at the point Lowry has called "closing denouement (in which the table of life gets set for us in a new way by the gospel)."[32] Hethcock is ready to close the sermon.

---

28. Hethcock, *Sermons Preached*, 67.
29. Hethcock, *Sermons Preached*, 67.
30. Hethcock, *Sermons Preached*, 67.
31. Hethcock, *Sermons Preached*, 68.
32. Lowry, *How to Preach*, 25, quoted in unpublished lecture notes, VTS, lecture 5, 2.

STOPPING: THE SERMON LENGTH IN A LITURGICAL SETTING

The best way to illustrate how important it is to stop preaching at the right moment is to quote the last paragraph of Hethcock's sermon:

> It may be that you and I will never be greatly affected by a scientist's discovery that iguanas shrink when they're starved, but I'm thankful that there is a scientist who was willing to suspend his committed assumptions long enough to make a new discovery. That scientist teaches me a lesson. If Nathanael had never been willing to look again at his traditional assumptions, he might never have known the Christ. Nathanael teaches me a lesson. You and I get stuck with our assumptions. We may need to give up what we believe in order to do what's right. It will take a little courage, but if we were to try this giving up our assumptions, I suspect we would find a great deal of God's truth around us we're missing out on.[33]

It is worth noting that several traditional elements are not there in the final paragraph of Hethcock's powerful sermon: "In conclusion"—not there; "Summary of points one, two, and three—not there; "Let us" or some other hortatory language—not there; "Amen"—not there. Hethcock maintains that the word "Amen" at the end of a sermon "has the effect of ending all thought and closing the subject."[34] The three essential elements of Hethcock's final paragraph are (1) a simple summary of the inductive process by which we arrived at the proclamation; (2) one main point, the sermon's proclamation, that states a fact: "We may need to give up what we believe in order to do what's right."[35] (3) This is then followed by a final gentle, yet powerful sentence that allows us to choose to accept and take away as our own the proclamation: "It will take a little courage, but if we were to try this giving up our assumptions, I suspect we would find a great deal of God's truth around us we're missing out on."[36]

---

33. Hethcock, *Sermons Preached*, 68.
34. Unpublished handout, VTS, "Invocations and 'Amens,'" 2.
35. Some might argue that the word "may" weakens this proclamation sentence and that imperative language (the mood of a verb expressing a command or exhortation) is more appropriate at the closing of a sermon. But here, the indicative (verb simply states a fact: "may need to give up") with the permission-giving "may" invite the congregation into accepting the proclamation, so that the sermon can keep working in the people's minds and hearts after the preacher has stopped speaking.
36. Hethcock, *Sermons Preached*, 68.

Hethcock follows his own advice about the sermon's place in a liturgical setting, referring to *The Book of Common Prayer* for the Episcopal Church as "the Prayer Book":

> The Prayer Book liturgy is simple and beautiful. It is decent and orderly. When we do what the Prayer Book says, our worship is clean and sense-making. When we add things, even some traditional things, we can allow our worship to become idiosyncratic, fastidious, and cumbersome. We can find ourselves inserting our own personality into the people's worship. The Gospel, then the response of the people, the preacher's opening words, the preacher's closing sentence, silence, "We believe . . ." [The Nicene Creed]; that is the Prayer Book order. I suggest that all who preach avoid adding to it.[37]

How long was the above sermon? My guess is it took 11 to 12 minutes because I can read it at an appropriate pace in that length of time. Hethcock says, "[T]he sermon should determine how long it should be. . . ."[38] I think this is his way of saying that the sermon should stop when it is finished. He notes that from five to seven double-spaced typed pages are within range for him.[39] I have found that speaking about 100 words per minute is a rate of speech that Southern congregations can follow easily, so 900 words (9 minutes) might be a little too short, and 1,400 words (14 minutes) would be a bit long in a liturgical setting. Hethcock writes, "A carefully planned sermon with a focus clearly in the preacher's mind when it was crafted in the study will move smoothly, carefully, and directly toward its proclamation so well that listeners will be unaware of its length. The sermon will end when the point has been made. Anything further damages the power of the sermon and makes the congregation become restless and even annoyed."[40]

---

37. Unpublished handout, VTS, "Invocations and 'Amens,'" 4–5; also unpublished handout, VTS, 3.

38. Unpublished lecture notes, SofT, hours 7–8, 1.

39. Unpublished lecture notes, SofT, hours 7–8, 1.

40. Unpublished handout #23, 2004, VTS, "Preaching at the Eucharist: A Talk Presented to the Preaching Excellence Conference, Virginia Seminary, June 5, 2000," 7.

PREACHING THAT SERMON FROM THAT SCRIPT

Hethcock's emphasis is on the "carefully planned sermon" that has been crafted in the study. For a new preacher, learning to trust that sermon script can be difficult. We may have been influenced by the notion that the Holy Spirit will speak directly to us at the time of sermon delivery. Indeed, Jesus assures us of the Holy Spirit's aid in time of trial (Matt 10:19–20, Mark 13:11, Luke 21: 14–15). However, those verses are intended to hearten early Christians as they stand before their persecutors. They are not license for the preacher to arrive unprepared in the pulpit and expect the Holy Spirit to supply a sermon script. Nor are they license to ignore the Holy Spirit's promptings all week long in favor of an impulsive moment in the pulpit.

An Oral Manuscript

Hethcock encourages using an oral manuscript. Oral manuscripts are typed in larger than normal point type with extra tabs, laid out in a manner that helps preachers to visualize and pace their delivery as they read sermons. Such a manuscript functions for the preacher as a score would function for a musician. This idea did not originate with Hethcock. He became aware of the concept in his teens when he read the sermons of Peter Marshall, who had been chaplain to the U.S. Congress. Marshall's wife, Catherine, compiled his sermons and copyrighted them in 1949 and 1950.[41] She made special arrangements to have them printed in 18-point Times Roman font and to copy her husband's oral manuscript format, as she explains in the book's Preface:

> Printed sermons are often as uninteresting as warmed-over potatoes. This is because they are designed to be heard, and are dependent on the preacher's personality for much of their effectiveness.
>
> In the pages which follow, these difficulties have been largely surmounted by the use of an unusual format. Peter Marshall always preached with a complete manuscript before him. These sermons have been set up just as his manuscripts were typed.
>
> Grateful acknowledgement is made to Dr. Trevor Mordecai, formerly pastor of the First Presbyterian Church of Birmingham,

---

41. Marshall, *Mr. Jones*.

Alabama, who first suggested this form to Dr. Marshall twenty years ago.

Originally intended for ease in reading, the style eventually became an integral part of Peter Marshall's work. It adapted itself to his vivid imagination and strong poetic streak.

On the printed page it conveys much of the force of his personality making articulate, almost audible, the written word. We believe that this style will add much to your reading enjoyment.[42]

Here is a sample of Marshall's way of laying out the words on the page of a sermon manuscript as the preacher might speak them from his sermon "The Paradox of Salvation":

They stood blinking at flashes of lightning
like daggers of fire.

There were eyes watching this Man on the Cross . . .
    shifting doubting eyes
        eyes through which Hell itself was looking
            eyes with gloating in them
                other eyes that looked and never saw.

Lips were moving . . . fierce fastened lips
drawn in thin lines of cruelty . . . open lips
that vomited blasphemy like craters of hate.

Faces were looking up at Him . . . white faces
        mad faces, twisted and distorted
        laughing faces . . . convulsed
        faces . . .
    faces jeering and roaring round the foot
        of the Cross.[43]

---

42. Marshall, *Mr. Jones*, 17–18.
43. Marshall, *Mr. Jones*, 146.

It is easy to see from this excerpt what the sermon might sound like as it is delivered. Hethcock introduced the notion of an oral manuscript to his students and offered some suggestions, but he did not require it. Most of what I learned about oral manuscripts came in a later homiletics class taught by J. Neil Alexander and, therefore, is not the subject matter of this work. However, I gradually adopted a similar technique that works for me, illustrated in the sermon at the end of chapter 2 and elsewhere in this book when I give examples from my sermons. Now, when I prepare a sermon manuscript, I find that it flows naturally in a stair-step manner (using tabs) as I type it. This visual manuscript helps me deliver sermons more effectively from the pulpit. The spacing helps me know when to pause and makes it easier to find my place again after looking out at the congregation.

Preachers can learn to use an oral manuscript, in which every word to be spoken has been written down, so that the manuscript is not obvious at all to the congregation and the sermon does not sound like a reading. Once the preacher is comfortable with an oral manuscript, it is much easier to trust the Holy Sprit's work in the study and to preach only that sermon from that script. In about ten years of preaching from a script, I have rarely had a truly original, spirit-inspired idea in the pulpit that did not come to me first in my study. A true inspiration can be vetted for its source in the study, where it is easier to distinguish between the voice of the Holy Spirit and the voice of our unholy egos. In addition, the preacher who uses a script can actually see how the sermon might be heard. How far back, for example, is the antecedent to that pronoun? Is "he" Jesus or Peter? How much time and diversion have gone by since I introduced that thought? The preacher who answers these kinds of questions in the study and then sticks to a script has a better chance of preaching an effective sermon that can be heard.

5

Making Your Way Through the "Guidelines" and Finding Your Own Modifications

A DOZEN OR SO years before we moved to Sewanee for seminary, Tom and I taught the middle school Sunday School class at our church in Alabama. My older son, Timothy, was in that class. One year we found a set of British street plays on parables and settled on one of them for the class to perform. The performance was to take place on Sunday morning in the allotted sermon time, and it began with Timothy standing up unexpectedly just as the sermon started and interrupting the preacher. The class was never able to present the play due to one complication after another that fall. The cooperating preacher became ill. Timothy's grandmother, who had been forewarned, breathed a heavy sigh of relief, and Timothy suppressed his desire to interrupt the preacher for the rest of that year.

A few years the other side of seminary, on a Christmas Eve that fell the night of the Fourth Sunday in Advent, Timothy arrived home. He had made a grueling winter-weather bus trip from Chicago to Alabama through snow and sleet. On the way, his luggage had been stolen. He'd arrived without most of his clothes and without the Christmas presents he'd packed to give the family. I wasn't ready for Christmas either as a priest or a mother. Preparations had been breathless. The congregation's usual routines had been interrupted because the Fourth Sunday of Advent was December 24th. No leisurely, party-like decorating of the church. No days of additional choir practice. Everything had been rushed and pushed into the tiny window of time between the end of the Sunday morning Fourth Advent service and the beginning of the Christmas Eve service—Christmas Eve dinner, choir practice, greening the nave. It occurred to me as I contemplated this unfolding scenario earlier in the week that this baby was coming early—no one was really going to be ready for Christmas, but God was going to come into our lives that night anyway.

So, I began the sermon that Christmas Eve with a rhetorical question, "Are you ready for Christmas?" and moved seamlessly from my presumed "No" into a theme of our lack of preparation but God's willingness to come into our lives, ready or not.

"Are you ready for Christmas?" I asked the congregation. From about four pews back Timothy's lone voice came in response to my invitation, releasing that long-suppressed desire to interrupt the preacher: "Yes," was his answer. I looked down at the sermon manuscript, which really should not be rewritten at that moment. It all depended on "No."

Hethcock's handout to the Sewanee seminary students, "Some Guidelines for Sermon Preparation," deals with questions from the pulpit. He says, "I suggest that you do not ask a question unless you either know what the answer will be in the minds of the hearers, *or* you are prepared for any answer."[1] Not every preacher is blessed with a son who speaks out loud the answer to a rhetorical question that turns out not to be what the preacher expects. Every preacher is probably blessed with members of the congregation who do not happen to think like the preacher does and who are going to have an answer to a rhetorical question bouncing about in their heads as the preacher heads off into the sermon, presuming the opposite answer. As the sermon is supposed to be about what the person in the congregation is hearing instead of what the preacher is saying, this disconnect causes a derailed sermon.

Hethcock presents other reasons for not asking questions: that the preacher may come across as "parenting" the congregation and the sermon will sound condescending, or that the flow of the sermon will be interrupted.[2] Instead of asking a question and pausing, he recommends that the preacher either gives an immediate answer to the question or converts the question into a declaratory sentence. I could have said, "Are you ready for Christmas? Some of us wonder if we are." Or, "I wonder if you and I are ready for Christmas this year." Either approach would have allowed me to move on, including my son and everyone in the congregation who were readier than I had imagined. "I suppose that guy

---

1. Unpublished handout, SofT. Hethcock used a modified version of this handout at VTS in 2004, which is reprinted in Appendix B of this book. In the VTS version, he deals with rhetorical questions in guideline no. 10.

2. Unpublished handout no. 5, VTS, see Appendix B, guideline no. 10.

who stole my suitcase needed it more than I did," my son had told me. Yes, Timothy might have been readier for Christmas than I imagined, even if the baby Jesus was coming early that year.

As Hethcock's sermon preparation guidelines are reproduced in Appendix B, they require little comment. Hethcock covers sixteen topics in the Sewanee handout and eleven in the handout for Virginia students. Many of the topics overlap. Reasons for his recommendations are clearly set forth, drawn from years of listening to and teaching preachers. "Every guideline," says Hethcock "is designed to get the sermon heard."[3] For example, the guideline on "Identification"[4] encourages preachers to select a biblical character with whom they hope the congregation will identify because, says Hethcock, "If I identify with blind Bartimaeus, then when he gets healed, I get healed, too. And, of course, blindness is a metaphor."[5] If the congregation begins to experience healing along with Bartimaeus, then the sermon has indeed been heard.

MODIFICATIONS TO THE GUIDELINES

By offering guidelines (Appendix B), Hethcock does not intend to discourage preachers from making their own judgments. "The guidelines are always going to be violated when they need to be violated," he says. "They are not rules or commandments. The goal is to shape the preacher so that he or she will be able to make sensible decisions about how to handle the sermon."[6]

Over the years, I have allowed myself some modifications that have worked for me. They may not work for you. In the following areas, I have listed my own modifications of Hethcock's recommendations:

Humor

Hethcock urges the use of humor "with great caution," sanctioning "mild humor" that is designed to help the congregation become involved in the sermon. He strongly discourages "raucous humor of the knee-slapper sort" and says that "humor designed to put the preacher at ease" is "al-

---

3. Interview with Hethcock, January 10, 2009.
4. Unpublished handout no. 5, VTS, see Appendix B, guideline no.2.
5. Interview with Hethcock, January 10, 2009.
6. Interview with Hethcock, January 10, 2009.

ways out of place."⁷ I do not disagree with these recommendations, but I have also come to appreciate a positive function of humor. It is to open the pathway to emotions, so that listeners can be more vulnerable to the depth of a proclamation. In this example from a sermon I preached on the prologue to John, I tried to use three funny stories to lead to the deeper concerns that underlie the humor and into the incarnation.

In the Episcopal Church for this Sunday
    we depart from the Revised Common Lectionary.

We leave off hearing about shepherds and angels,
    stories that invite us in and fire our imaginations.

Last week when we heard about the angel Gabriel
    making that auspicious announcement to Mary,
        a teenager at Otey Parish was so engaged
            that she leaned over and whispered
                something in the rector's ear.

Then when Father Ballard got up to deliver the sermon,
    he began by telling the congregation what she had said.
        "If Gabriel had come to visit me," she had told him,
            "I'd tell Gabriel,
                'OK, but you're the one
                    who has to tell my parents.'"

(The congregation laughed.)

Stories about these Christmas stories abound.
    Last week I got an e-mail about something that was supposed
        to have actually happened in an Episcopal Church.

During the annual Christmas pageant,
    the child assigned to play the innkeeper
        was having a really hard time
            telling Mary and Joseph there was no room in the inn.

---

7. Unpublished handout, SofT, "Some Guidelines for Sermon Preparation," guideline no. 6.

"That is how it happened,"
   the adults, the Sunday School teachers, his parents
      all told him.
         You have to say it that way.
            Your line is, "There is no room in the inn."

But when it came time for him to say his line,
   the child told Mary and Joseph,
      "There is no room in the inn,
         but won't you at least come in for a drink?"

(The congregation laughed more lustily.)

         It's an Episcopal Church, you see.
           And it is funny because it is
               a little bit of self-deprecating humor.

Yesterday I heard another one.
   This one was told by the Rev. Lee Lowery
      as part of his Christmas sermon
         at Holy Spirit Episcopal Church
            in Alabaster, Alabama.

(Note the intentional use of the exact same language of the previous story in what follows.)

During the annual Christmas pageant
   the child assigned to play the innkeeper
      was having a really hard time
         telling Mary and Joseph there was no room in the inn.

"That is how it happened,"
   the adults, the Sunday School teachers, his parents
      all told him.
         You have to say it that way.
            Your line is, "There is no room in the inn."

But when it came time for him to say his line,
   the child told Mary and Joseph,
     "There is no room in the inn,
       but you can come home with me instead."

(There was hardly any laughter.)

It's the Episcopal Church, you see,
   and the piece of Christian theology that is most central
        to us,
    that says the most to us about who we are
      is our understanding of incarnation,
        which is why we put our emphasis there
          every first Sunday after Christmas.

The Word became Flesh and dwelt among us.
   The Word set up tent with us,
     tabernacled in our flesh,
       took up residence in our own homes and bodies.

It is what makes us Christians.
   It is what makes that child's response
     to the Christmas story so completely right.
       There is no room in the inn
         but you, Christ, may come
          and make your home with me.

We are a frightened and confused,
   harassed and troubled people.
     We are losing jobs and homes.
We are worried about health insurance and taxes.
   We wonder if the money we have been saving
      for college or retirement will be there when we need it.
       We worry about the next natural disaster
         or the possibility that terrorists will attack again.

We worry about our daughters
 when they become pregnant,
  about our loved ones who despair,
   about those who are battling illness,
    about those we love who drink too much,
     about those who are off far away from family
      trying to make us more secure.

All of that is going on when the angels and shepherds
 come to us each Christmas.
  And then the poetry of John
   breaks into the Christmas story line.
(Now the congregation is ready to go deeply with me into incarnation and what it means to us.)

Questions[8]

Even though I have admitted to learning the wisdom of this particular guideline the hard way, I feel free to make my own modifications. Questions still occur in my sermons, particularly a string of related questions spoken in such rapid fire as not to allow mental answers but serving as title or transition to the next thought. One Advent I asked,

How do we live in preparation for the coming?
 How do we do that when we have no idea when or how God's
  purposes will finally be fulfilled in the coming of Christ?
   Are there hints of such preparation, even deep under the tinsel
    of our commercial world, upon which we can shine a light?
    I think so.

I asked those questions with no expectation that anyone would actually be searching for immediate answers, rather, with an expectation that the congregation would follow me into an exploration of the hints of preparation that might lie deeply under the tinsel.

---

8. Unpublished handout no. 5, VTS, see Appendix B, guideline no. 10; unpublished handout, SofT, "Some Guidelines for Sermon Preparation," guideline no. 13.

Personal Stories[9]

Hethcock discourages using personal stories, primarily because they draw attention away from the Gospel and toward the preacher. He suggests telling the story in the third person. In his handout for Sewanee seminarians, he even discourages use of the first person singular pronoun altogether, saying "Try to preach without using the word 'I.'"[10] Barbara Brown Taylor offers a somewhat different perspective when she says that if she uses the word "I," she hopes the congregation will say, "me too."[11] I find that personal stories or stories about friends or family *used sparingly*, not as the main fare each Sunday, bring an authenticity that allows the sermon to be heard as the preacher's offering of some truth. Often the preacher is not the subject of the story but the observer.

Following immediately after the "I think so" answer to the three rapid-fire questions in the sermon above, here is a piece from that same Advent sermon that I hope illustrates effective use of a personal story:

I grew up in what I will call a Christmas family.
  Maybe you did, too.
    There was nothing in the year, no birthday, no holiday,
      no family gathering, that was anywhere
        nearly as important as Christmas.

My father was, shall we say, "over the top" about Christmas.
  In some years, my father and I would take over
    the bay window in our ranch house.
      Using colored cellophane and black electrical tape
        we would create our own Nativity triptych
        —arguably acceptable in Advent.

But the silver tinsel Christmas tree that hung from the ceiling,
  rotating at an angle, turning red, now green, now blue,
    smacked of 1960s tasteless commercialism.

---

9. Unpublished handout no. 5, VTS, see Appendix B, guideline no. 4; unpublished handout, SofT, "Some Guidelines for Sermon Preparation," guideline no. 7.

10. Unpublished handout, SofT, "Some Guidelines for Sermon Preparation," guideline no. 7.

11. Taylor, *The Preaching Life*, 79.

Early every year, by which I mean sometime shortly after Easter,
> my father would begin thinking about Christmas presents.
>> By mid-summer he had his plans under way.

They could not wait for Advent.
> Four short weeks was just not enough time
>> to do something like find a jeweler who would convert
>>> the gold from the teeth he'd had removed years ago
>>>> into a stunning original pendant for my mother.
>>>>> Some things take thought, imagination,
>>>>>> Time, and research, not just money.

Every year my brother and I would receive one special present
> we had wanted all year long,
>> not something that showed up in late fall advertisements.

It was the unwrapped present we found on Christmas morning.

"Papa," I started saying early in 1960,
> "if I had a tape recorder with a microphone,
>> I could practice the lines for the plays I am in
>>> and work on my diction."
>>>> "A tape recorder!" he would interrupt,
>>>>> "You think money grows on trees?
>>>>>> No telling what that would cost."

But he was listening.
> He was listening for my heart's desire,
>> just like he did every year,
>>> long before Christmas, long before Advent.
>>> He was getting ready.

Without trivializing our practice of preparing for Christ's coming,
> I want to suggest that under the glitter of that silver Christmas tree
>> the morning I found the tape recorder,
>>> there was a metaphor,
>>>> a small reflection of the kind of preparation Advent requires.

Not long after the first Easter,
> Christians began preparing for the second coming of Christ,
>> looking and listening for its signs.

I wonder what Advent would look like if not long after every Easter
> *we* began listening for that coming,
>> calculating not when we might be beamed up into Christ's presence,
>>> but rather, calculating how we might cobble together
>>>> some of our excess gold to create a gift of love,
>>>>> trying to find out our Lord's heart's desire for us,
>>>>>> so that we would be ready at his coming
>>>>>>> with just the perfect gift.

By the time we gathered for Lessons and Carols,
> we could have spent the spring and summer listening
>> for what the bidding prayer tells us rejoices our Lord's heart—
>>> that we remember in Christ's name the poor and helpless,
>>>> the cold, the hungry, and the oppressed,
>>>>> the sick and those who mourn,
>>>>>> the lonely and the unloved.

And by Christmas morning, we could have lived much of the year
> in preparation for Christ's coming, not to snatch us away,
>> but to leave us behind in the world for which he died,
>>> which he loves, which he bids us care for,
>>>> and into which he will come again,
>>>>> so says the Bible,
>>>>>> so claims our faith.

We are every Advent nearer to that coming,
> the day and hour of which no one knows,
>> but for which we are called every Advent
>>> to watch, to wait expectantly, to listen, to prepare.

Quotations[12]

"Quoting is tricky," Hethcock told the Sewanee seminarians in the fall of 1997.[13] He was and is ever so correct. The congregation cannot see the quotation marks, and it is difficult to tell when the preacher has started or stopped using someone else's words. If you quote from sources other than the Bible in your sermons, following Hethcock's guideline about how to do this is very helpful.[14] He concludes this guideline with a caution about quoting directly from a book in the sermon. "Reading from a book in the pulpit is deadly. You will lose everyone. I recommend that you never take a book to the pulpit and read from it."[15]

Actually, my modification does follow the guideline because even though I have used a book on a few occasions, I have not taken it "to the pulpit." I've read from a book when preaching without a manuscript in an informal setting, standing on the floor at the same level with the people, in a church small enough for everyone to see and hear. (See the next modification on non-manuscript preaching.) When the preacher is standing among the people, the book is obvious, and the transition from the preacher's words to the words of the book's author need not be explained. I use long quotations from a book at times when only the author's actual words will carry the meaning and when the quote cannot be effectively shortened, times when I am willing for the sermon to be carried more by an absent author than by me. I once used a long section from Garret Keizer's *A Dresser of Sycamore Trees*.[16] I used this during a sermon from the floor on the story of Jesus meeting the disciples on the road to Emmaus (Luke 24:13–35). I had the book in my hand so the congregation could clearly see when I was preaching and when Keizer had written. The section is a series of beautifully told stories about home Communions. Only Keizer's words would do. The last home Communion in the section ended with an unexpected exit by the woman of the household:

---

12. Unpublished handout no. 5, VTS, see Appendix B, guideline no. 5; unpublished class handout, SofT, "Some Guidelines for Sermon Preparation," guideline no. 8.

13. Unpublished handout, SofT, "Some Guidelines for Sermon Preparation," guideline no. 8.

14. Unpublished handout no. 5, VTS, see Appendix B, guideline no. 5.

15. Unpublished handout no. 5, VTS, see Appendix B, guideline no. 5.

16. See Keizer, *A Dresser of Sycamore Trees*, 54–55, beginning with "Some of those I visit . . ." and ending with "'For the Communion,' she said."

> Perhaps the most memorable of these preparations [for Communion] occurred in a slowly collapsing house which I was visiting for the first time. I asked the woman if she and her husband, who was then suffering from dementia, would like to have Communion. She said she thought that would be nice, especially for her husband, who was not able to get to church. Then, without a word of explanation, she walked out the front door.
>
> After several moments she still had not returned. It suddenly occurred to me that she had taken my offer as an opportunity to step out for a while, perhaps to run some errands. Her husband seemed to get the same idea and was growing visibly agitated. What is more, I was supposed to be leaving for a long trip within the hour, and I could hardly leave the man alone. Why do I always get myself into these messes? I thought. To the best of my ability I assured the man that I was "coming right back" and went to the door to see if I could sprint up the street and catch his wife.
>
> But she had not gone. There she was, bending over in a weed-ridden vacant lot across the street. Was she sick? What on earth was she doing? Back she turned, grinning at me, with a bouquet of wild flowers in her fist. "For the Communion," she said.[17]

Yes, that is an extreme example. The full quotation (620 words) is about half the length of a normal sermon for me. This is not something I would recommend more than "once in a blue moon." But, later in the week when the senior warden told me of the connection he had made between those Emmaus Road traveling disciples recognizing Jesus at the table and that woman with the bouquet of wild flowers coming back from the vacant lot for the Eucharist, I thought it was a sermon that was definitely heard, even though it was more Garret Keizer's sermon that day than my own.

Manuscripts[18]

Between Sewanee and Virginia, Hethcock seems to have softened his recommendation about manuscripts. For my class he said, "At the School of Theology, we recommend that you use a manuscript and that you continue to use one as a preacher at all times after seminary."[19] He drops that absolute in Virginia but still emphasizes the virtues of using a

---

17. Keizer, *A Dresser of Sycamore Trees*, 54–55.

18. Unpublished handout no. 5, VTS, see Appendix B, guideline no. 9; unpublished handout, SofT, "Some Guidelines for Sermon Preparation," guideline no. 16.

19. Unpublished handout, SofT, "Some Guidelines for Sermon Preparation," guideline no. 16.

manuscript. In ten years of preaching, I have followed this advice at least 95 percent of the time. His reasons (clarity, control of the sermon, reduction of anxiety) become more and not less persuasive week in, week out. However, there are times when it is effective to preach without a manuscript, and I have modified this recommendation.

When might it be more appropriate to preach without a manuscript? In small churches when fifteen to twenty people show up on Sunday morning, standing behind a raised pulpit and addressing a congregation sprinkled five or six pews back is, at best, awkward. On what may be the most memorable day in a couple's life, a few words spoken directly to the bride and groom, overheard by the congregation, may have much more impact than a well-crafted, twelve-minute sermon they must take in by looking up from the first pew to a pastor who is towering over them. The same can be true at a funeral.

Finally, for festival occasions of the church like Easter and Christmas, the sermon is best kept very short so that the liturgy dominates, and the resurrection or the incarnation may be better represented out among the people. One Easter Sunday morning in a church that did not yet have an Easter Vigil, we were baptizing a young girl. As she sat on the front pew, she had become shy and slid down between the kneeler and the seat to crouch on her stepfather's feet. This was the lectionary year of the reading from Mark with the short ending; no resurrection is mentioned. It stopped, "and they said nothing to anyone, for they were afraid" (Mark 16:8).

I decided to stand in the aisle among the people and wonder, under those circumstances, how the Word got out. As the sermon wound to its conclusion, I noted that the Word kept getting out because it was being passed when Johnny told Bobbie (on the right side of the aisle), then when Bobbie passed it to up to Julie (in the choir loft in the back) and when Julie came to church and shared it with Barbara, who passed her faith in the Word on to Katherine (back down onto the nave floor and this time on the left side of the aisle), so that now the Word was out and would land on someone we were baptizing that morning. At that point, the little girl sprang up like a jack-in-the-box and squealed, "That's me." The Word might have happened the same way to that congregation if I had been behind a pulpit with a manuscript, but somehow I think joy burst out because the congregation and I were engaged in the sermon in a way that allowed a little piece of resurrection to be experienced. Every now and then, maybe, not being completely in control of the sermon seems appropriate, and when the topic is resurrection, it may be more appropriate.

That said, the preacher does not need to work at *losing* control over the sermon. The sermon still needs a focus sentence and still needs to be guided by a clear idea of where the preacher is going and how. A few things help me. First, it is a good time to remember Lowry's "then and then and then." If the sermon has a plot, it can be told just as if it were a story. Second, those memory tricks we have learned along the way actually do work. I sat for the bar exam in 1977, and I never practiced much property law. Nevertheless, I can still tell you that the classical elements of adverse possession are "Open Continuous Exclusive Adverse and Notorious" because I doubt one can adversely possess the "ocean," though the oceans and seas certainly can be adversely affected. Remembering that is effortless. I would have to try to forget it.

Sermon moves that spell out key words or proceed in alphabetical order or can be imbedded in alliteration that is not obvious go a long way toward preventing anxiety. Third, a note card in the alb pocket provides security even if I never look at it. A built-in excuse to look at the note card, to get the words of a quotation exactly right, for example, provides an opportunity to see key words that cue the next move(s). For particular occasions, proclamations from the floor can be effective as long as they are not considered the only "real preaching" and as long as they are exceptions to the rule of preaching from a manuscript.

6

Making Your Way Through "Feedback"

Hethcock contends beginning preachers do not necessarily learn to preach better just by preaching. They can improve their preaching, however, by receiving and acting upon feedback that is helpful. Addressing the need for preaching feedback as a part of seminary education, Hethcock writes, "Merely preaching over and over does not insure growth in skill; the feedback component from trained listeners is critical for the process to be fruitful."[1]

Before Hethcock began teaching homiletics in 1984, he was the field education director for the School of Theology at the University of the South in Sewanee, Tennessee. In that capacity he began listening to students preach in "preaching groups" and offering critiques, long before he actually began to teach preaching. When he began to teach preaching, the idea of feedback groups was already in place. Hethcock also trained his students in how to listen and comment on the sermons of their fellow students.

A preaching group consisted of from six to eight students. After a fellow student delivered a sermon, which was usually recorded on camera, the students and Hethcock would jot down their thoughts on a form Hethcock had provided. The first question required the students to write the preacher's focus sentence. Discussion then began, with each student stating the focus sentence as he or she had heard it. For the student preacher, this feedback made it clear whether the intended proclamation had been received.

Over the years, I have received a good bit of feedback after services at the church door, but none of it has begun, "I think your focus sentence this morning was . . . ." Indeed, the first time I preached outside the seminary, I received feedback that was both common and uncommon. I was engaged in "Clinical Pastoral Education" at a hospital, something

---

1. Hethcock, "Looking Again," 94.

Sewanee seminarians do after the first year before any training in homiletics, although Hethcock had met with us for one introductory session. That morning members of the congregation were sitting in wheelchairs spread out under florescent lights, yet positioned to allow them to gaze through full-length sliding glass doors into the adjacent lawn, which is what my first sermon critic had been doing. As she rolled up to me after the service, face beaming, and extended her hand, I heard what is probably the most common compliment preachers receive. "Sister," she said, "I sure enjoyed your message this morning."

Then the feedback turned uncommon. Before I could smile politely and shake her hand, she kept going. "Of course," she went on, "I did not hear what you were saying because when I was getting ready to come down this morning, I could not for the life of me find my hearing aids. And, my eyes are not too good so I didn't see you up there either. But, I sure did enjoy being here." Perhaps this was a reminder to me to pause and to remember that, after all, it is God's message—not our own—we preachers have to offer. That woman's uncommonly honest feedback reminded me that whatever fruits our own efforts bear or fail to bear, God is still at work. Frequently, those who show up for church seem to "hear" a proclamation they need to hear, whether or not it bears any relationship to what the preacher has said.

When we begin to serve as priests, ministers, or deacons who are expected to preach every Sunday or on a regular schedule in large churches, receiving useful feedback is still helpful if we are to continue preaching effectively. Congregational feedback can be useful but cannot be handled in exactly the same manner as seminary classroom feedback. While the logistics are more difficult than we might imagine, as preachers we can ask members of the congregation to give us feedback informally, or we can organize a preaching feedback group that meets at a designated time after the Sunday sermon has been delivered. In a seminary preaching group, as soon as the preacher has stopped, other students begin recording their feedback. That can never be done in a congregation unless members of a feedback group take notes during the sermon. That is probably not a good idea because it is distracting to the rest of the congregation and unnatural for the listener. It is hard to be engaged emotionally or experientially if the intellectual task of note taking demands most of the listener's energy. Also, congregations typically finish Sunday services around lunchtime, so if the preaching feedback group is to meet immediately after the service, the group probably needs to have snacks. It is hard to fill out a feedback form and eat, and harder yet to delay socializing with other members of the group while eating. The preacher may be needed in another location, such as the after-service coffee hour. But the longer the time span is between the sermon's delivery and giving the feedback, the less valuable the feedback will be.

The other primary problem in congregational feedback is training the listeners in what to listen for and how to make useful comments. If you are new to a church and it already has a sermon feedback program, be sure to meet with the group early on and let them know what types of feedback you find helpful. Congregational members may think their task is to comment on the preacher's theology, but this is rarely what they need to do. Their task is further complicated if those in the feedback group are unfamiliar with how the preacher has been trained, so give them basic information on your preaching style. If the church has no feedback program and you want to ask some parishioners to participate in a feedback group, before the group ever meets for a post-sermon session, gather together to get to know each other, agree on the group norms, decide how the listening and feedback will be done, and be sure that the group understands what will be useful to you.

Starting with the format Hethcock used with his seminary students, he later designed a process for congregational use. We tried the process out at Otey Parish in Sewanee in 2007 with a field education student preacher, using Hethcock's instructions, titled "Giving Field Ed Students Feedback on Sermons," and the written evaluation form he designed, "A Form for Evaluating Sermons"; both are in Appendix C. At the end of this process, Hethcock wrote up his recommendations for designing, instructing, and working with a preaching feedback or listening group in a congregation. These recommendations are Appendix D, "Talking Back to the Preacher."

A preacher who wants to establish a feedback group should select members who intend to be helpful, who can accept the proposed guidelines for the group, and who are not predisposed to be overly critical. The group would exist to support, encourage, and improve the ministry of preaching. During seminary field education, I found my feedback group quite helpful, as did the Otey field education student in 2007. A feedback group need not be permanent or even long term. For example, it could be set up for a season of the church year with an evaluation of the process at the end of that season. Appendices C and D provide a preacher with excellent resources for establishing and training such a group, resources that are not simply the preacher's ideas; therefore, they could be accepted as expert recommendations on how to give feedback.

Epilogue

How Using the Hethcock Process Can Make Us Better Preachers

IN 2004, WILLIAM HETHCOCK told his class at Virginia Theological Seminary that his four-step process is not perfect. He explained that his process of preparing to write a sermon is intended to move preachers beyond simply giving a lecture: "We want scripture to touch the experience[s] of the persons in the congregation. You are not preaching until that happens. Remember, the work of the sermon is to bring the hearers, the congregation, to *experience* the truth of the Word of God—the Gospel of Jesus Christ—in the context of the worship of the Church."[1]

Back at Sewanee early in his teaching career, Hethcock tells of talking with a student outside class when she said, "I've got to go write a sermon, and I don't have any idea where to start."[2] Hethcock designed his four-step process for those of us who often feel like that student, to help us to move from "I don't have any idea where to start" to bringing the congregation to "experience the truth of the Word of God—the Gospel of Jesus Christ"—as they worship. While Hethcock draws on the work of many in the field of homiletics, his design of the four-box process is unique because it can be used every week as a framework for preachers to analyze 1) the meaning of the biblical text; 2) a human condition there and then, inside the text and inside the early community the text addresses; 3) a similar human condition here and now, among those the sermon will address; and 4) the essence of the text that can be proclaimed to the congregation. After the preacher works through this thought process and writes down answers to questions in each of the boxes, he or she is then ready to begin to compose the sermon.

---

1. Unpublished lecture notes, VTS, lecture 1.
2. Interview with Hethcock, May 30, 2008.

I can speak for myself but not for other preachers in answering the question of how working through Hethcock's process has helped me. While it would be interesting to identify preachers among Hethcock's students who use this process and ask them to reflect on this question, such a survey is outside the scope of this book.

The process had greater value when I first began preaching and had no idea where to start. In later years, sermon preparation has become more intuitive. However, I still find value in continuing to use Hethcock's process. The principal value is that the process provides a straightforward, uncomplicated template that requires me to mine the scripture and make the necessary connections between the scripture reading and the people it first addressed and then the scripture and the people in the congregation for whom I will preach. I make these connections before I begin to think about what I will say in my sermon or how I will say it. The template steers me away from the temptation to begin sermon preparation with some intriguing observation, illustration, metaphor, or idea of my own. Hethcock's template is only one page (see Illustration 2 in chapter 2). I keep it stored as a file on my desktop to use whenever I need to prepare a sermon. Although at first I had to study how to use that template and what is involved in each of its boxes, once I began using it week in, week out, I could move through the process without having to refer to anything other than the template, my Bible, and a few reliable biblical commentaries for the exegesis.

This process requires that I proceed through the exegetical step and then examine and match up the human condition in three separate places. After I have followed the steps in all four boxes and not taken any shortcuts, I have made the necessary connections between the scripture and our lives. Only then am I ready to start writing my sermon. I have confidence that the connections I have made are among those intended by the original evangelist because I have explored the human condition of the people for whom that evangelist was writing. Then, I should be able to articulate how the scripture touches our lives before I decide on a focus for the sermon.

As I've found a clear connection between the scripture and our human condition in this preparation process, my finished sermon will have a good chance of bringing the experience of the Word of God into our worshipping community. It is extremely important for me not to skip any of the human condition steps in the boxes for "then and there" and "here and now." Skipping one of the human condition steps compromises the proclamation. For example, focusing only on a "here and now" human condition could import concerns into the biblical text that may have nothing to do with the text itself. On the other hand, focusing only on a "then and there" human condition can lead to a proclamation that is informational but devoid of contemporary impact. Hethcock's understanding of "supportive confrontation" (see chapter 3) happens best when the scripture is allowed to touch a properly identified human condition that is grounded in the biblical text, present in the early Christian community, recognized in myself (the preacher first), and then in this particular congregation.

Going forward into preparation of the sermon itself, the process focuses and disciplines my creativity without discouraging it. The way I use the process, there is a place in it for deciding upon and developing metaphors (see chapter 2) and narratives (see chapter 4). Then when it is time to write the sermon script, I know I will usually start within the identified human condition, as it is disclosed inside the biblical text, or through a narrative, or by a metaphorical image I have chosen. After I start writing the sermon, developing it is much like pulling one or more threads until it or they come to a point of connection between the scripture and the human condition, to proclamation, and resolution.

Additionally, Hethcock's guidelines for actual preparation of the sermon (see chapter 5 and Appendix B) have given me some clear indications of how the sermon might be heard, even when I choose to modify them or not to follow them at all. Indeed, I was unable to find a sermon to use as an example in which I followed all the guidelines; yet, I am aware of these guidelines and make decisions based upon them as I compose each sermon. The exemplary sermon I selected for this book (as Appendix E) is one preached by Hethcock in 2009 at Otey Memorial Church in Sewanee, Tennessee.

As I have practiced this process over the years, I hope I have delivered effective sermons that have been heard. Indeed, with faith and practice, I hope that those of you who have been inspired by this book to use this process will find that you have become instruments through which your congregations can actually experience God's Word—Christ's Gospel—in the context of worship. In this book, I have sought to preserve enough information about Hethcock's process so that those of you who make your way through it may be helped to start "really preaching."

Appendix A

An Annotated Bibliography of Biblical Resources for Preaching[1]

COMMENTARIES

Brown, Raymond E. *The Anchor Bible.* 2nd ed. *The Gospel According to John.* Vol. 29, chapters I–XII. Garden City, NY: Doubleday, 1986. First published 1966 by Doubleday.

———. *The Anchor Bible.* 2nd ed. *The Gospel According to John.* Vol. 29A, chapters XIII–XXI. Garden City, NY: Doubleday, 1985. First published 1970 by Doubleday.

Every preacher should own and use this. Fr. Brown includes his own translation and verse by verse commentary plus articles on some subjects. Each volume includes useful appendices, and an index in volume 30 covers volumes 29, 29A, and 30.

———. *The Anchor Bible.* Vol. 30, *The Epistles of John.* Garden City, NY: Doubleday, 1982.

I rarely preach on these letters, so I rarely use this commentary. At the same time, Fr. Brown is so dependable, and this volume is so inexpensive that if I didn't own it, I would buy it.

Bryan, Christopher. *A Preface to Mark: Notes on the Gospel in Its Literary and Cultural Settings.* New York: Oxford University Press, 1993.

Professor Bryan stresses literary analysis as a means of exegeting the text. Chris is my good friend, and he has guided me to understand this means of interpreting scripture for more effective biblical preaching. [Professor Bryan is the C. K. Benedict Professor of New Testament, Emeritus, at the SofT. Though Bryan has retired, he continues to

---

1. William Hethcock recommended these resources to his seminary students at the School of Theology at the University of the South and at Virginia Theological Seminary. Comments and updates added by Jerrilee Lewallen are in brackets.

teach courses in New Testament and to serve as editor of *The Sewanee Theological Review*.]

———. *A Preface to Romans: Notes on the Epistle in Its Literary and Cultural Setting*. New York: Oxford University Press, 2000.

This book is tougher going than Chris' Mark volume (above), but it is good reading for a better understanding of Paul for preaching. I am using it to help me turn to Romans more often as a preaching option.

Craddock, Fred B. *John*. In the Knox Preaching Guides series, John H. Hayes., ed. Atlanta: John Knox Press, 1982.

This is a simple, scholarly, down-to-earth commentary that is very useful in preaching on John. Professor Craddock is a trustworthy and exciting exegete we can always depend on. It is out of print; the SofT library has a copy.

Grieb, A. Katherine. *The Story of Romans: A Narrative Defense of God's Righteousness*. Louisville: Westminster John Knox Press, 2002.

This is a new book that I have not examined thoroughly. However, I have read a number of other works by Professor Grieb, and I find her down to earth and helpful. I look forward to more use of this volume.

Harrington, Daniel J., S. J., ed. *Sacra Pagina*. Collegeville, MN: Liturgical Press, 1991–.

I have only the four gospels, but a complete set would include all the books of the New Testament. The authors translate each pericope and follow with verse by verse commentary and a section entitled "Interpretation," in which is given additional exegetical information helpful to preachers. [This is a 17-volume set. Harrington is the general editor; each volume has a different author.]

Interpretation: A Bible Commentary for Teaching and Preaching. Louisville: John Knox Press, 1982–.

Rather than verse by verse, commentary and interpretation for preaching are composed concurrently. The scholarship seems dependable, but it is not intended to be thorough or detailed. This reference complements rather than replaces your more scholarly commentaries. I often find it very helpful. (Similar commentaries on the Old Testament are available, but I don't have them.) [Each of the seventeen volumes covers one book of the New Testament and has a different author.]

Käsemann, Ernst. *Commentary on Romans*. Translated and edited by Geoffrey W. Bromiley. Grand Rapids, MI: Wm. B. Eerdmans Publishing Co., 1980.

This is a good, basic, heavy-duty commentary on Romans, helpful in preaching and in leading Bible study. Alas, no two commentaries agree on Romans (actually, I haven't seen them all), but this one is competent and helpful, a good guide when we're making up our minds how to say it in the pulpit.

Long, Thomas G. *Matthew*. In the Westminster Bible Companion series. Louisville: Westminster John Knox Press, 1997.

Professor Long, formerly at Princeton, now at Candler, is a fine scholar and deservedly noteworthy homileticist. This is not a profound book, but it is *very* helpful for Year A preaching, especially when Matthew gets to be rough going. I highly recommend that every preacher own a copy.

New Interpreter's Bible, The. Nashville: Abingdon Press, 1994–.

Twelve volumes cover the entire *Bible*. Every pericope is included in both the New International Version and the Revised Standard Version. A detailed commentary follows, although not always verse by verse, and "Reflections," which suggests possible interpretations for preaching. I have found this set *very* helpful. For those who don't want the whole thing, volumes VIII and IX, which contain the four gospels, would be a good buy. Parts of the twelve volumes are available on disks; presumably eventually the whole set will be. This purchase would be a big savings in both money and shelf space. My understanding is that an index, which would be very helpful, is forthcoming. [An index volume was added in 2004. A commentary on each book of the *Bible* is written by a different scholar.]

Schweizer, Eduard. *The Good News According to Luke*. Translated by David E. Green. Atlanta: John Knox Press, 1984.

———. *The Good News According to Mark*. Translated by Donald H. Madvig. Richmond: John Knox Press, 1970.

———. *The Good News According to Matthew*. Translated by David E. Green. Atlanta: John Knox Press, 1975.

A very helpful set of basic scholarly commentaries on the Synoptic Gospels. Translations of Scripture are from, for some reason, *Good News for Modern Man: The New Testament in Today's English*. You'll find verse by verse commentary with extended remarks on some pericopes. Each volume has an informative introduction. I find these quite helpful for preaching and Bible study.

> Wright, Tom (N. T.). *John for Everyone*. (2 vols.). London: Society for Promoting Christian Knowledge (SPCK), 2002. The 2nd edition was published as a paperback by London: SPCK, and Louisville, KY: Westminster John Knox Press, 2004. [The other books in this series followed the same publication process except the book on Acts, which was first published by both publishers.]
>
> ———. *Luke for Everyone*. 1st ed., 2001; 2nd ed., 2004.
>
> ———. *Mark for Everyone*. 1st ed., 2001; 2nd ed., 2004.
>
> ———. *Matthew for Everyone* (2 vols.). 1st ed., 2002; 2nd. ed., 2004.

[In addition to the books Hethcock lists in this series, these are also available:

> ———. *Acts for Everyone*. (2 vols.). 2008.
>
> ———. *Hebrews for Everyone*. 1st ed., 2003; 2nd ed., 2004.
>
> ———. *Paul for Everyone*. (7 vols.). 1st eds., 2002, 2003; 2nd ed., 2004.]

These are small, simple, paperback commentaries with sermon suggestions on every text in the Biblical book indicated in the title. They are relatively inexpensive and fairly useful. I find them useful about half the time I look something up.

Lectionary Commentaries for Preachers

Most publishing companies specializing in biblical materials furnish an extensive commentary on the Sunday readings according to *The Revised Common Lectionary* [RCL]. This lectionary was published by the Consultation on Common Texts, which included liturgical scholars from sixteen Protestant denominations and the Roman Catholic Church. The Episcopal Church and the Anglican Church of Canada were among the participants.

These volumes do not contain sermons. Their value is that they can "jump start" preachers in the direction of crafting their own sermons in ways that might not occur to them on their own. This can be especially helpful to someone who is preaching every week.

[The Episcopal Church began considering adoption of *The Revised Common Lectionary* in 2000. In 2006, at its 75th General Convention, the Episcopal Church adopted *The Revised Common Lectionary* to replace the lectionary in *The Book of Common Prayer*. Congregations were given a period of time to implement this change. Hethcock's comments below precede that development.]

There are two additional reasons for owning and using one or more of the following publications:

1. Even though the RCL is different from our 1979 BCP Lectionary, it is close enough for the articles to be helpful on almost every Sunday, and

2. The forthcoming General Convention will consider making this the official lectionary for our Prayer Book.

Note: It [the RCL] is approved at present for use in congregations who have gained their bishop's permission. Clergy who are concerned with enriching their biblical preaching should consider requesting such approval and experimenting with this lectionary.

> Brueggemann, Walter, Charles B. Cousar, Beverly R. Gaventa, and James D. Newsome. *Texts for Preaching: A Lectionary Commentary Based on the NRSV*. Year A, vol. 1. Louisville, KY: Westminster John Knox Press, 1995.
>
> Brueggemann, Walter, Charles B. Cousar, Beverly R. Gaventa, and James D. Newsome. *Texts for Preaching: A Lectionary Commentary Based on the NRSV*. Year B, vol. 2. Louisville, KY: Westminster John Knox Press, 1993.

Cousar, Charles B., Beverly R. Gaventa, J. Clinton McCann, and James D. Newsome. *Texts for Preaching: A Lectionary Commentary Based on the NRSV*. Year C, vol. 3. Louisville, KY: Westminster John Knox Press, 1994.

I find the articles in these volumes insightful, competent, and useful.

> Craddock, Fred B., John H. Hayes, Carl R. Holladay, and Gene M. Tucker. *Preaching through the Christian Year*. Philadelphia: Trinity Press International, 1992. (Three volumes, one each for years A, B, and C.)

This is my favorite, and I always go to it first. The reason is that Professor Craddock, who is responsible for all the gospel commentaries, is always reliable. His very sensitive pastoral insights into exegesis usually touch my own thinking to get me going.

> Fuller, Reginald H. *Preaching the New Lectionary: The Word of God for the Church Today.* Collegeville, MN: The Liturgical Press, 1974.

Interestingly, [now, the late] Professor Fuller, an Episcopalian [who had] retired from the faculty of VTS, wrote this commentary on the Roman Catholic version of the lectionary for use by their clergy before our Prayer Book was published. Although it is sometimes helpful, its brevity is its limitation.

> Sourds, Marion, Thomas Dozeman, and Kendall McCabe. *Preaching the Revised Common Lectionary.* Nashville, TN: Abingdon Press, 1992–1994. (Twelve volumes in paperback, four for each of the years A, 1992; B, 1993; and C, 1994.)

This is where I go if I seem to be "stuck." Sometimes I am quite surprised by the creative "take" an author will have on a given reading.

> Van Harn, Roger E., ed. *The Lectionary Commentary, Theological Exegesis for Sunday's Texts.* Grand Rapids, MI: Wm. B. Eerdmans Publishing Co. and London: Continuum, 2001.

Three volumes, one each for the First, Second, and Gospel readings. (E.g., the Old Testament and Acts reading for all three years are in one volume, etc.) These are fairly new, published in 2001. The articles have been solicited from a great variety of authors. They tend toward very scholarly, exegetical help and less toward specific ideas for sermons. I find these books very useful, and I refer to them often.

[The following series is a recent addition in this category of commentary:

> Bartlett, David L., and Barbara Brown Taylor, eds. *Feasting on the Word: Preaching the Revised Common Lectionary.* Louisville, KY: Westminster John Knox Press, 2009.

This new series comes in four volumes per liturgical year. Each lesson for each lectionary has the text (NRSV) followed by four perspectives: theological, pastoral, exegetical, and homiletical, written by dozens of contributors who are scholars and/or pastors. Preachers who use Hethcock's process as described in this book may find the pastoral perspective helpful in identifying the "human condition."]

Periodicals Including
Lectionary Commentaries for Preaching

Periodicals with all new commentaries with every issue are vast in number, as the collection in the seminary library makes evident. I will mention (with some prejudice) only two below. What we really need is a directory of online commentaries, but at this point I have been unable to put together such a document. [A number of online resources are now available with links to commentaries, articles, and sermons. One I (Lewallen) use regularly is *The Text this Week: Lectionary Scripture Study and Worship Links and Resources*, nondenominational resources compiled by Jenee Woodard, and can be found at www.textweek.com/.]

Anyone who wants to subscribe to a periodical commentary should examine the library collection while still in seminary where a good collection is available. Each person must decide on the basis of cost and personal suitability.

Synthesis: A Weekly Resource for Preaching and Worship in the Episcopal Tradition. This is the only periodical I know based on the Prayer Book's 1979 Lectionary. Delivered monthly in a packet containing a four-page folder for every Sunday and important feast day. Page 1 contains biblical commentary; page 2, historical or traditional information on the reading; page 3, person reflections and cultural information from one of the editors, plus hymn and service music information using *The Hymnal, 1982*; and page 4, one or more brief sermons on the readings by the editor-in-chief, often from a social action perspective. Two concerns of mine: this is a relatively expensive publication, and it sometimes includes material that I do not find helpful. You might be able to purchase any three volumes above or four gospels in the *NIB* set (2 volumes) for the same amount or less. [The new title of this periodical is *Synthesis: A Weekly Resource for Preaching and Worship following the Revised Common Lectionary*. An ongoing publication, *Synthesis* changes with time. The editors of *Synthesis* have also created a three-volume series for years A, B, and C of *The Revised Common Lectionary*.]

Tuesday Morning: Resource for Ministry and Liturgical Preaching.

Published quarterly for $20 per year based on the RCL. Contains brief articles of interest to preachers plus commentaries for every Sunday and important feast days. Somewhat uneven because of different authorship of each commentary but usually helpful.

Appendix B

HANDOUT 5

Various Guidelines to Consider in Writing Your Sermons from Hethcock's 2004 Class at Virginia Theological Seminary

1. INTRODUCTIONS

Some people continue to have introductions to their sermons setting the scene, getting the congregation relaxed, or otherwise sort of "cranking up." They want to establish the congregation's interest in what the sermon will be about.

> The scenario is sort of like this. The Gospel has been read, the preacher is in the pulpit, the people have said "Praise be to thee, O Christ," and they are ready to listen.

I recommend that you jump into the sermon right away with no crank-up introductory material.

You will be wise to establish the track of the sermon as near to the beginning as you can.

Begin where you want them to listen.

Sunday, Proper 25, Year B (Mark 10:46–52) is about the healing of the blind man, Bartimaeus.

> Focus Sentence: Jesus the Christ calls us to open our eyes and dare to see his Gospel even though it may challenge what we already know.
>
> Function Statement: To bring people to awareness of our self-imposed blindness in favor of our status quo religion.

Possible Opening: I read an article recently about a man who after a lifetime of blindness was, through remarkable surgery, given his sight. Everyone was so happy for him. How fortunate that he could receive this miracle! He could look at his wife and children for the first time. He could see the world around him. His whole life was changed.

But what the article said is that the newly received sight, rather than being the blessing all assumed it would be, was actually an enormous burden for the man. The adjustment was tremendously difficult for him.

The difficulty was that he couldn't recognize anything. If he saw an orange, he had to close his eyes and feel it to know what it was. If he saw a tree, someone had to tell him that that is a tree. He was often sick with a nervous stomach because the barrage of colors and the intensity of light were so shocking, so unusual.

We can't imagine what it would be like suddenly to be given the gift of seeing after years of blindness.

This man we're hearing about this morning, Bartimaeus, has been blind for his whole life. He has lived a life of begging. His life is one of complete darkness, and doubtless he has become used to it. And then suddenly, Jesus touches him, and the man sees Jesus and all the crowd around them at once. We have to wonder what he must have thought.

I even wonder whether the shock of this sudden seeing comes to the man as a good thing.

Sunday, Proper 18, Year B, (Mark 17:31-37) is about the healing of the deaf mute.

Focus Sentence: Jesus the Christ calls us to open our ears and dare to hear his Gospel even though it may challenge what we already know.

Function Statement: To bring people to awareness of our self-imposed deafness in favor of our status quo religion.

> Optional Opening 2: I knew a woman who could scarcely hear at all. She had a damaged eardrum, and her hearing was seriously impaired. I talked to her one day just after she had visited an ear specialist in a neighboring city. He was planning a surgical experiment, the grafting of skin to build her a new eardrum, and in preparation for this procedure, he had made a temporary eardrum of paper.
>
> The woman was a nervous wreck. Suddenly she was able to hear things she hadn't heard in years. Driving home, she had feared that her car was malfunctioning because she had never heard its noisy engine. Every time her dog barked she jumped. Her children were driving her crazy with just normal behavior. She wasn't sure that this being able to hear was going to be so great after all.
>
> I have to wonder how happy this deaf and mute man in Mark's Gospel really was at suddenly being able to hear.

Start where you want to, but get the track of the sermon under way very early.

An introduction in the classical sense is probably unnecessary—a waste of time.

You are more likely to lose your listeners with an introduction than with an immediate entry into what you want to say.

2. Identification

Identification is not something a preacher needs to talk about, but it is something of which the preacher needs to be aware.
In almost all sermons, there is someone with whom you intend the people in the congregation to identify.

This is very subtle. You describe this person carefully so that people will understand this person and eventually begin to think to themselves that they are like that person in some way. Or that they have feelings of empathy for that person.

> This sermon on Proper 25 is eventually going to call on people to identify with deafness.
>
> Blindness is a metaphor here, and the only way my proclamation will work is for everyone to share in being blind in a metaphorical sense.

> The reason I want them to identify with the blind man is that when I reach my proclamation, I want them to be vulnerable to it.

For the proclamation to touch where they are, they must admit to a metaphorical blindness.

> I am going to describe his blindness. He does not see what's going on around him. He can stay focused on himself, because his own misery is the only misery that comes to his conscious mind. His blindness is very convenient, because at all times he can claim to miss something he doesn't want to see by saying in an apologetic way that he is, after all, blind.
>
> You and I are blind. When it suits our purposes, we don't see a thing. It is very difficult to attract the attention of an American these days because we Americans are afflicted with a self-imposed case of blindness. You can talk and explain and point out and warn and advise if you want to, but we're not listening, not when someone is trying to revise the comfortable outlook, the positive-thinking world view that we have so carefully constructed for ourselves.
>
> The question we come to is this: do you and I have the courage to ask Jesus to give us what we think we want? Jesus says, "What do you want me to do for you?" Dare we say, "Lord, I want to receive my sight"?

By making a metaphorical use of blindness, I am calling on you in my sermon to identify with him.

Sometimes you have to shift the identification from one character to another.

Two men went into the Temple to pray, one a Pharisee and the other a Publican.

> I may design this sermon so that the congregation identifies with the Publican. But then, we are also like the Pharisee. And so . . .
>
> I am trying to avoid that "either-or-ness" I was talking about during Friday's discussion.

We had some of this in our discussion of Mary and Martha. I may invite the congregation to identify with Martha, deal with that, and then invite them to identify with Mary.

This is a word of caution: Generally speaking, it is never good to try to ask the congregation to identify with Jesus.

We want them to identify with the person who is acted upon by Jesus.

Then too, Jesus is holy and divine. How can I identify with that?

> This is my argument with WWJD [What would Jesus do?].
>
> Jesus would never be in the mess I'm in, so the more appropriate question is a question of ethics.
>
> What would Jesus *have me* to do? His life and teaching are my guide, not his personal decision making.

3. Illustrating the Sermon

Everyone will want, from time to time, some story or illustration to include in the sermon that will help the point of the sermon to be clearer.

The illustration most often illustrates either the exegesis or the human condition, and sometimes, it illustrates both.

O. C. Edwards, Jr., a prominent, though now retired homileticist, used to make model airplanes out of kits that came with a block of balsa wood.

The plans showed the shape of the fuselage of the plane, for example, and you just kept working on the piece of wood until it was the right shape.

You held it up to the template until it was precisely the right shape. The sermon illustration is like that.

You work on it until it fits just right.

The move in and out of the illustration is very tricky. "That reminds me of . . ." is a little obvious.

Just pause and move into the story, finish it with clarity, and move out of it.

A story that requires a good deal of explanation to make it fit doesn't work.

> *But some appropriate work must be done to make sure and certain that the congregation understands how the story illustrates what you're talking about.*

The illustration must be of the appropriate [emotional] strength.

An illustration that is too strong will eclipse the sermon, that which is being illustrated, and, therefore, will do more damage than good.

> Illustrations about cancer or serious illness are dangerous. You never know who in the congregation is suffering from an illness or who may discover an illness in the next week.
>
> Illustrations that include family tragedy, especially the death of a child, are usually too strong.

Alcoholism, drugs, derelicts, and the like usually do not work. Bishop Duval watched the building of the stone parts of the conference center at Kanuga.

The stone masons chose just the right stone to go into the place that needed the stone next.

This is Bishop Duval's illustration of how to choose an illustration: Chose the stone that fits right where you need to put it.

Canned illustrations tend not to work for me.

Some preachers save files. I don't find them helpful.

A plan for thinking up an illustration:

What do you want the illustration to do? What will be the "work" of the illustration in the sermon? Can you describe it?

What instance or situation in experience or literature, news media or general conversation, seems to be like what you would like to illustrate in the sermon?

> What is the power of the image you have discerned? Will it work in the context in which you need it?
>
>> Is it strong enough?
>> Is it *too* strong?
>> Feel free to edit your images.

You do not have to be 100 percent honest. You don't want to use an image that everyone knows and edit that, but you are free to take the story and do what you have to do to it to make it work in the context in which you need it.

Of course, you can't edit literature, especially works that are recognized.

4. Personal stories

Generally speaking, talking about yourself and your family in a sermon is very bad form. Using members of your family or yourself as examples of this or that is very bad form. Telling personal stories about yourself and your experience is out of place.

Parishioners will tell you that they want to know you and that they like hearing about you and your family.

They mean it when they say it.

The truth is, however, that your personal stories get old, and people get tired of hearing them.

> *They draw attention to you as the preacher, and you are supposed to be speaking the Gospel on behalf of Jesus Christ, not promoting your own popularity and well-being in the congregation.*
>
> *If you preach from your heart and share your faith, people will get to know you without having a good deal of personal data.*

I will admit that there may be an occasion when a personal experience is what you need in the sermon.

Ask the question, "Will this story work in the sermon—will it do what I need it to do—if I tell it in third person as if it happened to someone else?"

If the story absolutely will not work unless you explain that it involved you or happened to you or your family, then, of course, you have to make it a personal story.

> The story about the woman who was going to have a grafted eardrum was my mother. There was no need for me to tell you that in the sermon.

A priest I know in Texas constantly told stories about his childhood in Virginia.

They were long and involved stories, and the people in Texas had very limited interest in their priest's family, boyhood, or relatives in Virginia.

Texans have very limited interest in Virginia!

> The stories rarely clearly illustrated what the priest was talking about.

Another preacher I heard said, "I've been asked not to talk about my grandchildren, but I want to tell you this story anyway."

He had even been *asked* not to do it, and he was still doing it.

> In this instance, the congregation was not only weary of hearing about his grandchildren, but the preacher also was inadvertently distancing himself from young adults in the congregation who have no grandchildren. He made them aware that they were listening to an old man.

5. Quotations

Everyone wants to quote someone at one time or another.

The best rule is, in general, don't use quotations.

A quotation, especially a long one, will be in the style of the person whom you are quoting. The cadence of your speaking will change. The change in cadence, tone, and style of language is disruptive to the flow of the sermon. Rather than helping, quotations very often actually are distracting and disruptive to the preaching.

> It is very difficult for people to hear a long quotation read to them in the context of preaching.

The reasons are subtle. They have to do with sound, cadence, word choice, syntax, and all the other things that make the way you and another person speak and preach unique.

There are exceptions to the general guideline.

When the quotation is very short:

"Humphrey Bogart in his role as Rick Blaine in 'Casablanca' warned, 'I stick my neck out for nobody.'"

"Martin Luther King, standing there in front of the Lincoln Memorial, held his huge audience spellbound when he began his sermon, 'I have a dream!'"

"Jimmy Stewart in his role as Elwood Dowd listened patiently to his psychiatrist warn him that he had to be more realistic. Dowd responded, 'I've wrestled with reality for thirty-five years, Doctor, and I am happy to say I have finally won out over it.'"

If you have a quotation that you really want to use, and it is important to you, do it this way:

a. Tell the people what the quotation is about and what it says in advance.

b. Read the quotation.

c. Paraphrase the quotation in your own words, making sure that the reason you are using it is clear.

> In this way, you profit by the quotation and what it has to contribute to your sermon without breaking your cadence or surrendering your own voice.

The best thing to do is to paraphrase the quotation in the first place, rather than using a direct quotation, especially if it is long.

Feel free to paraphrase a quotation in your own words.

Reading from a book in the pulpit is deadly. You will lose everyone. I recommend that you never take a book to the pulpit and read from it.

6. Using the present tense

Most of the time in our preaching we want to retell the Bible story.

Some preachers object to this. They say that the story has already been heard by the people and that it is redundant or perhaps insulting to retell it.

They would probably be right if we retold the story exactly as it appears in the Bible reading for the day.

But the retelling of the story is a way to introduce your exegesis into the sermon.

You don't tell the story exactly as it has just been heard.

You tell the story in the light of your exegetical work, putting the slant on the story you want the congregation to hear to move them toward what you want to proclaim.

> The retelling uses different words, which will help them hear your interpretation of the pericope.
>
> The retelling may well drop out some part of the reading that will not be useful to you in the sermon.
>
> The retelling will weave into the story information that perhaps is not in the text, but it will be helpful to the understanding of those hearing it.

When we are retelling the Bible story—and consistently throughout the preaching—we use the *present tense*.

The rationale for this is that the preacher wants to make the ancient text immediately applicable to and relevant to the experience of the congregation.

Telling the story in the present tense allows the story to sound brand new, here and now, in the moment.

We believe as preachers that this ancient text is new every day; using present tense helps to make this belief true.

Sometimes by way of transition, a preacher may be heard to say, "Now, what does all this that happened 2,000 years ago have to do with us today?"

What a disastrous remark! The answer might well be, "Nothing at all."

The language of the preacher will do well to close the gap of time and make the movement from Jesus' presence with his disciples or Paul's letter to his friends or whatever the scripture is by merely stepping from one scene to another in one step.

Reminding the congregation that the Scriptures are ancient gets in the way of helping them to see the biblical message to be immediately relevant.

7. About "ought" and "should"

What we need to say about "ought" and "should" is that they are almost never helpful in addressing the congregation in the sermon, especially in the proclamation, the ending.

I like the word "can" as a way to speak of God's enablement at the end of a sermon.

We might sometimes say, "You and I can find ourselves able to. . . ." Or, "The Spirit brings power to us so that we will be enabled to. . . ."

A possible ending to the sample sermon mentioned before on Proper 25, Year B, (Mark 10:46–52) might be:

God is standing by this morning waiting to heal our blindness and to give us sight. On the surface, the prospect is promising, good, worthy, peacemaking. But below that surface, we want to protect ourselves from seeing what Jesus' message really means. Because we know when we do see in Jesus' terms, we will be changed, and we will hear a call to see the real world more bravely than we dare.

What you and I can do, rather than becoming afraid of God's demands, is trust in God's loving presence. That trust will teach us that we have nothing to fear from truly seeing and that in truly seeing there is joy and fulfillment in knowing the Gospel message and speaking it bravely.

8. Knowing and doing

Every sermon should end leaving the congregation with something to *know* or something to *do* or something both *to know and to do*.

In Anglicanism, "knowing" sermons are typical because the sermon will be followed by a compelling liturgy.

> The liturgy is going to say, "Send us out to do the work you have given us to do."

If we are preaching to help people change and grow, then knowing sermons have their place.

The people come to church not only to know something new, but perhaps also to be ready to incorporate the "new knowing" into their spiritual outlook so that change can happen.

> When the sermon ends, we have been informed, our faith has been challenged, we have heard the Gospel proclaimed in a new way, and we are otherwise called on by the sermon to *know* something.

> This is especially true of a doctrinal sermon, such as you might preach on the Incarnation at Christmas or on the Resurrection at Easter.

A sermon on a missionary focus, an outreach focus, for example, might call for some action, something a person should *do*.

Remember that when you are preaching in the context of the liturgy, the liturgy will make its claim, its demand on the people. You are free to make a statement that touches the spiritual nature, the knowing and worshiping nature of the people, without enjoining them to action every time you preach.

A balance between the two would be a good idea.

9. Manuscripts

The question of whether a preacher should use a manuscript in preaching is a widely debated subject among teachers of homiletics and other preachers.

Some argue that there is no way to catch the attention of a congregation if a manuscript is used.

I recommend and urge you to use a manuscript.

I am aware that many, perhaps your field site supervisors, will urge you not to use a manuscript, but I think, especially at this point, preaching without a manuscript is an error.

Further, the requirement that everyone speak without a manuscript presupposes that everyone is equal in skill when actually some memorize easily, and others only with difficulty.

> Especially early in one's preaching career, not using a manuscript only adds another dimension of anxiety, which is not helpful.

Some preachers who are urged not to use a manuscript or who decide not to use a manuscript will craft sermons to be spoken without any aid, and they will be less serious, perhaps even somewhat trivial.

Using a manuscript well is a skill we can learn.

We can learn to use the manuscript without appearing to be reading and without allowing the manuscript to impede the kind of contact with the people the preacher desires.

There are some things you can do that will help you use a manuscript in your preaching without its being intrusive or cumbersome for you.

Especially with a computer, you can design a manuscript that is helpful to your own personal needs.

Then you can practice your sermon with your manuscript until you know it well enough that you are not looking at it constantly. You can have eye contact with the congregation.

People in your congregation who say they want you just to talk need to make a change in their outlook.

Fred Craddock says that this effort to get preachers to preach without notes or manuscript is a part of the contemporary American anti-intellectualism. He has a point.

10. Questions

Preachers debate whether questions are helpful in a sermon.

The flow of listening to a sermon can be interrupted by the preacher's asking questions, especially if they are asked under the guise of "making the congregation think."

If you are preaching with some consequential content in your sermon, they are listening. Asking them questions—"What does all this mean?" or "What do you suppose is going on with Jesus?" or "What do you think Peter means by that question?"—comes across as the preacher's parenting the congregation, which is demeaning and insulting.

Some preachers are using these questions to make a transition from one part of the sermon to another.

When this is happening, placing the question in a declarative sentence helps.

> Instead of asking, "What does all this mean to us?" say instead, "What we really want to know is what all this means to us."

> This announces what is coming next, namely, your answer to the question raised by what has gone before.

Similarly, "What do you suppose is going on with Jesus?" might become "Jesus is puzzling us, and we wonder what's going on with him." And "What do you suppose Peter means by that question?" might become "When Peter asks a question like that, we wonder what he means." Each of these suggestions is designed to bridge to the preacher's answer to the questions just raised.

11. Appropriation by Listeners

Whatever the proclamation proclaims must be something the listeners can appropriate into their own thinking and doing.

The here-and-now human condition you have identified in the sermon may be so serious that as we listeners hear it, we feel helpless.

The ending, however, must be something that we can know or do that moves toward change.

There is no point in leaving a congregation convinced of the truth of the condition you have described but unable to respond.

Every sermon has to be reasonable in terms of whether we can actually appropriate it into ourselves as listeners.

The appropriation does not have to be easy, of course.

Challenge is appropriate and desirable. But it does have to be reasonable, possible, and achievable, or the congregation will reject it.

> No one wants to be left by the sermon feeling helpless or guilty.

Appendix C

*Giving Field Ed Students Feedback on Sermons
and A Form for Evaluating Sermons*[1]

GIVING FIELD ED STUDENTS FEEDBACK ON SERMONS

"Feedback" (or "critique") is information we receive from others following an act of speech or writing on which we desire a descriptive assessment of content and form or delivery. Generally speaking, feedback should only be given when it is requested, although there are structured learning situations in which giving and receiving feedback are parts of a learning design.

The small homiletics listening group is a learning design that depends upon giving and receiving competent feedback to accomplish its goals. An individual preaches a sermon at the morning service(s), the members of the group listen, and when invited they respond with their feedback.

The person giving feedback *always speaks from a personal point of view* with *thoughts* and *feelings* about specific language, structure, and delivery of the sermon. No one can speak for others in the listening group. It is permissible, however, for a group member to agree with an aspect of another member's evaluation occasionally, but at all times feedback must be given from the personal point of view of each listening group member.

Feedback proceeds from the thoughts and feelings of each listener. One speaks with helpful feedback when saying, "When you spoke of President Bush in the language you used, I felt angry because it sounded disrespectful to me." The respondent is addressing a specific moment in the sermon with personal feelings and the reason for them. Such feedback is good and helpful. It would not be appropriate to say, "Everybody

---

1. This information and form were designed by Bill Hethcock for a listening group at Otey Parish in Sewanee, Tennessee, January 2007.

knows that you have no business criticizing our president that way because it is un-American and unpatriotic, and you ought to know better." This group member is using generalities that are unhelpful to the preacher. The individual seems to be trying to justify his/her own feelings by passing them off as everyone else's. Group members need to speak using the first person, "I," not the third person, "everybody" or "they."

When we give negative feedback, we also speak in the first person with our thoughts and feelings. The statement is always a factual observation. For example, helpful feedback might be, "When you told the story about the drunk in the barroom, I thought it sounded unrelated to your point and out of place in your sermon." It is not helpful to say, "The story about the drunk in the barroom was silly and confused and offended everyone in the room."

In all instances, feedback needs to be given with care and sensitivity. Even negative feedback can be given in a way that will help the preacher become more skilled and effective at delivering sermons. Honest feedback given in a considerate manner should always prevail. Being dishonest, for example, complimenting an aspect of the sermon that the listener actually thought was unhelpful is detrimental to the preacher's learning process and could encourage the preacher in a way that impedes growth.

The person receiving the feedback, the preacher, has the right to determine whether what has been said is helpful or unhelpful and whether or not the information conveyed by listening group members will be used in future preaching.

A FORM FOR EVALUATING SERMONS
BY FIELD ED STUDENTS

Preacher _____

Listener _____

Date _____

What is the one point you heard the sermon making?

What other information unrelated to the one point did you hear?

To what extent did you sense yourself becoming involved in the sermon? Mark a point on the scale that best represents your answer.

Not involved at all									Very involved
1	2	3	4	5	6	7	8	9	10

How did the preacher's language and word choice *help* or *hinder* your understanding of the sermon?

Describe any stories, images, or illustrations that *helped* or *hindered* your listening and understanding:

How did the verbal or physical aspects of the delivery *help* or *hinder* your listening and understanding?

What elements of the sermon contributed to its being effective?

What might the preacher do to present a more effective sermon next time?

(Use the reverse side of the page as needed.)

Appendix D

TALKING BACK TO THE PREACHER

*A Manual for Lay Persons
Who Want to Evaluate Sermons*[1]

Contents

Why Evaluate Sermons?
The Overall Plan
Getting Started—Forming the Group
Getting Started—Orienting the Group
How to Give Constructive Feedback
The Listening Group Agenda and Process
About Feedback Sheets
Sample Feedback Sheet A
Sample Feedback Sheet B
Sample Feedback Sheet C
A Quotation about Sermon Critique

---

1. William Hethcock, D. Min., Sewanee, Tennessee, third edition, 2008. © William Hethcock

WHY EVALUATE SERMONS?

Clergy who preach to congregations, especially when they preach every Sunday, genuinely want to know how they are doing. They often wonder whether their sermons are being heard by their congregations in ways that strengthen their people, inform them, and challenge them to move in new directions with stronger faith and commitment. Every preacher appreciates the generous compliments received at the back door after the service. However, these remarks are often so general and good-hearted that they do not give preachers genuine guidance on whether their sermons are effective in terms of what they intend their preaching to accomplish. There is no way, based on this kind of feedback alone, for the preacher to learn and grow.

At the same time, there are listeners in the congregations of these preachers who are not only ready to hear the gospel preached to them every week, but who are also competent to give constructive evaluation to their preachers. They listen carefully, and they generally appreciate the hard work and good intentions of those who preach to them. They have responses kept within themselves that would be helpful to their preachers if only there were a means of discussing them openly and forthrightly.

This manual is conceived with the assumption that if information about the sermon were to flow between listeners and preacher, not just as pleasant words, but as well-intended, constructive critiques, all would benefit from the conversation. *Talking Back to the Preacher* is designed to facilitate this communication between preacher and congregation with a view to assisting the preacher to learn more about how effective he or she is and how growth and improvement in preaching may come about. The people in the pew may also learn how better to listen to what is being said to them from their pulpit.

THE OVERALL PLAN

The setting for this conversation about the sermon will include the preacher and six or seven appointed lay responders meeting as soon as possible after the sermon is completed for perhaps one or one-and-a-half hours. The sooner the session can take place, the better the chances of fresh information being exchanged before feelings and other data begin to escape from memory.

Those who have been listening to the sermon will respond both on paper and orally. The plan discourages any conversation among a few of the listeners before all come together with the preacher. All feedback will be more effective if it is shared in the presence of the preacher and the listeners together at the same time.

Someone other than the preacher should be appointed to facilitate the conversation by making sure that all feedback is clear and that everyone has a chance to speak. The preacher should participate as a group member rather than the leader, so that she or he will be free to listen and respond without having an assigned duty.

GETTING STARTED—FORMING THE GROUP

The preacher may form the listening group in either of two ways—by appointing the entire group or by appointing a leader/facilitator who, in turn, assembles the other five or six members. Six or seven persons in addition to the preacher will make the ideal number in the group—not so many that members' "air time" during the discussion is limited, but not so few that an inevitable absence of one or two will limit good feedback and varying points of view.

Where there are multiple clergy staffs with more than one preacher seeking feedback, there should be a separate group for each preacher. If the same group were to critique the sermons of more than one preacher, the membership would likely find themselves comparing one preacher with another. Even if this comparison were not verbalized, its presence in their thinking would inhibit complete freedom to speak about the sermon at hand. Each preacher should be encouraged to grow in his or her own preaching, free from competition, real or implied, with other staff members. "No one can serve two masters," observes Saint Matthew (6:24). One group endeavoring to serve two or more preachers will have some difficulty forgetting the absent one to focus on the preacher in the room.

From time to time, the group may discover itself serving as a support group for the preacher to whom it gives critiques, particularly as that preacher requests and receives feedback of a more personal nature. If a standard of confidentiality evolves, it should be unencumbered by conversations with other preachers.

GETTING STARTED—ORIENTING THE GROUP

Before the group can begin to hear a sermon and give feedback to the preacher, the members need to participate in one or more meetings with the preacher, who will orient them to the job they will be doing.

First, the preacher must spend some time telling the group members how he or she goes about crafting a sermon. The error most often made in giving critiques is that the information is not related to the specific intentions of the recipient. More about how our feedback may be most helpfully worded will come below, but here we need to know that "shotgun-like" critiques are not very helpful. What is the preacher intending in the crafting of sermons that the listening group may look for and address with specific data? What strategy is the preacher using to help the congregation listen and hear? Presumably every preacher has a plan (sometimes called a process, method, or routine) of sermon preparation with specific goals for his or her preaching. The group members' individual feedback should address the effectiveness of that plan. They should specifically note where the preacher's ideas, words, delivery, and all else the preacher intends to communicate are accomplishing or failing to accomplish what the preacher intends.

The preacher's sermon may have an introduction, may use stories or images, may ask questions, or may need comments on the ending or closure. The preacher may point out these or other features of the sermon for which feedback is especially needed. Of course, group members will identify other characteristics of the sermon they think would be helpful to discuss with the preacher.

The group members need to hear the preacher discuss his or her theory of biblical interpretation or exegesis. Presumably in biblical preaching, the preacher has a personal approach to interpreting scripture and proclaiming the biblical message from the pulpit. What is that approach and how does it influence preaching?

For example, in the Personal Profile almost all Episcopal priests keep updated in the Church Deployment Office in New York, each clergy person has checked one of six points on a series of continuums between two stated extremes. Under a section entitled Regarding Theological Views, the continuum on how the priest uses the Bible has on one end "Regards the Bible literally" and on the other end "Regards the Bible as an interpretation of God's dealings with humanity." Responding to this question, the priest will check one of the six blocks.

The group members critiquing he sermon will be helped by knowing where their preacher stands on biblical interpretation, how she or he goes about it, and how that interpretation informs a given sermon.

The preacher may well decide during this orientation to bring to the group a video or audio recording of a sermon recently preached. (If neither is available, a manuscript of a sermon will serve.) The preacher can help the group members by showing them how the sermon is constructed, why it is constructed that way, and what idea or point was meant to be proclaimed to the congregation. For example, the preacher should show how what was said from the pulpit was intended to lead the thinking of the people to a new experience of the gospel. When the group members are "on board" with the preacher's strategy for developing a plan and an intended message, they will be better equipped to give feedback when the time comes. The preacher may have some handouts that will give on-going assistance to the listening group members.

The second component of the group's orientation is hearing how to give feedback and experimenting with their own language in order to be the most effective and useful to the preacher. When one or more members have experienced a negative response during the preaching, rather than withholding this important information from the preacher, they need to know how to give it in a constructive manner.

Carl Rogers, a noted psychologist of the mid-20th century, used to comment, "The facts are always friendly." What he meant is that the bad news we come to know about ourselves and our work is actually good news, because knowing when something is amiss enables us to do something about it. All the feedback that group members can give about the sermon, positive, less positive, and negative, constitute good news for the preacher, who can do nothing about any of them until he or she knows what they are.

The third component of their orientation is giving an outline for the process the group will follow when it begins to do its work.

HOW TO GIVE CONSTRUCTIVE FEEDBACK

Feedback is information we give to someone (or even to a group) to indicate how that person's behavior—language and actions and words—affect us as observer-listeners. Feedback in listening groups is usually verbal, but during sermons nonverbal feedback might include laughter, applause, a sneer or yawn, or even walking out of the room. Feedback as we are using it here is intended as information that can be used for improvement, and for the most part it will be verbal and written.

Unless we are aware of how best to give feedback to someone who has just preached a sermon, we can actually do harm. This danger can sometimes prevent us from giving any feedback at all. The same danger causes others to say only "nice things." Members of the sermon listening group need to develop the skill of giving both good news and bad news in a helpful and supportive manner about what they have heard in the preaching.

Sermon listening groups' feedback can have three helpful effects:

1. Feedback may confirm the preacher's positive behavior by encouraging its repetition.

    "The way you tell the biblical story helps us feel like we're right there on the scene."

2. Feedback may help bring aspects of the preacher's delivery or sermons' content in line with what the preacher intends to convey to listeners.

    "If you could keep your volume up and avoid dropping your voice, we could hear you more clearly."

3. Feedback may help a preacher eliminate a distracting behavior.

    "I had trouble following your main theme because the sermon makes so many different points." Or,

    "I found myself having difficulty listening because of the way you rock back and forth when you preach."

The best feedback is worded as "I-messages." Whenever possible, each group member will do well to address the preacher beginning with "I." This means that the group members report their own thoughts, feelings, and opinions that occurred as they listened to the sermon. Beginning with "I," the speaker is owning (that is, taking responsibility for) his or her feedback in a way that allows the preacher to hear it more as a gift of helpful critique than as possibly damaging criticism. The I-message shows that each group member intends to give support to the preacher and to the preacher's learning and growth.

Some criteria for giving feedback guide us toward offering what we have to say in genuinely useful ways:

- Feedback is always *descriptive* rather than *evaluative*. By describing one's own reaction, feedback leaves the preacher free to use it or not to use it as he or she likes.

    Evaluative: "I like the way you use your voice."

    Descriptive: "I think that allowing the volume and the pitch of your voice to vary according to what you are saying helps to keep the congregation engaged."

- Feedback is always *specific* rather than *general*. The preacher can use specific feedback to make positive changes, whereas general feedback is impossible to apply effectively. The group members will be most helpful when they identify the exact point in the sermon to which their feedback makes reference.

    General: "I kept getting confused during the sermon."

    Specific: "I became confused when you were comparing the two men praying in the temple."

- Feedback is always *appropriate* rather than *destructive*. The group member giving the feedback always intends to critique the preacher's sermon helpfully rather than harshly with destructive words or opinions.

    Destructive: "I don't see how you could miss the obvious similarity in the Old Testament words this morning."

    Appropriate: "While you were preaching, I was thinking that mentioning the Old Testament reading might strengthen your gospel message."

- Feedback is always *usable*. The preacher is only discouraged when something is mentioned over which he or she has no control.

    Unusable: "I could hear and understand you better if you spoke to us without that Yankee accent."

    Usable: "I could hear and understand you better if you spoke less rapidly."

- Feedback is always *timely*. The listening group members will do well to discipline themselves to report all they have to say to the preacher during the designated meeting time. At the end of the meeting, the conversation should be over. This discipline will prevent further conversation when the data has become cold and feedback will be less accurate and helpful.

- Feedback is always *clear* and *accurate*. Everyone, preacher and listeners alike, is responsible for making sure that all communications are understood during the time of the meeting. No one should leave the meeting saying, "I wonder what Tom meant by that." Group members may ask other members to explain a word or phrase they do not understand.

It is important for the preacher, who in this design is the one receiving the feedback, to have a chance to "check out" the feedback that is being given. This means that when one group member has made an observation, the preacher may take time to ask whether others in the room have the same perception. Sometimes all other members will say to the preacher that they did not make the same observation as the first speaker, in which event the preacher may safely decide not to use the feedback. More frequently, however, others will make the same observation or will edit the feedback with their own slightly different or additional perceptions. Such feedback is valuable to the preacher.

This practice of "checking out" the feedback helps the preacher to learn more about how the sermon was received in the congregation. The ways in which the preacher may act on the feedback are expanded.

A good idea is to practice giving feedback with the video, audio, or manuscript copy of a previous sermon brought to the training group by the preacher. All group members may then discuss their practice feedback and how each has given it. They will find themselves becoming better prepared for their first real session with the preacher.

THE LISTENING GROUP AGENDA AND PROCESS

The listening group should assemble with the preacher as soon as possible in a comfortable room apart from the telephone or other distractions. They should all be able to see each other when they speak.

It is appropriate for someone to be appointed to say an opening prayer. The preacher may want to ask someone to take notes so that he or she will have a record of what is said and will be free to enter into the conversation without encumbrance.

The session begins with a quiet time during which each listener fills out a feedback sheet. In spite of the temptation to laugh and talk, all should remain silent until everyone has finished writing. Actually, it would be even better if these sheets were available before the service so that they could be completed immediately after the sermon.

No group should decide to omit this step. The information recorded privately and before any conversation is the freshest response of the listener. The sooner it is written, the better. Even if it is necessary to delay the meeting for a day or two, which is less desirable, this feedback sheet should be completed right after the sermon is preached.

Having written down what they think before the conversation begins will protect each opinion from being influenced by someone else's words. While it is not inappropriate for opinions to change during the session, when possible, new opinions always need to be informed by these first impressions and ideas recorded on the feedback sheet. Not to include a feedback sheet and not to give time for its completion as the first agenda item would seriously damage the value and accuracy of the feedback available to the preacher!

If each group member has been faithful to the task of completing the feedback sheet, each will have recorded in one sentence what she or he heard as the point communicated by the preacher.[2] When the sentences fed back to the preacher are alike or highly similar to the preacher's intended point and to each other, it may be assumed that

---

2. This manual assumes that all preachers who use it are given to the discipline of preaching only one-point sermons. No popular method of sermon preparation currently encourages preaching more than one point. The rationales for this rule vary, but most homileticists teach that, because of the way we listen, contemporary listeners can hear only one point. When the sermon includes two or more points, all points come across as weaker and are quite likely not to be heard at all.

the preacher has communicated the intended point effectively. The degree to which these sentences vary or are actually dissimilar will indicate the degree to which the preacher's point was not clearly communicated.

On occasion, listening group members may feed back to the preacher similar points they have heard that are actually specifically unlike the preacher's intended point. They may have heard a "secondary point" that detracts from the intended authority of the preacher's predetermined main point. In these instances, the preacher can learn that there is something amiss in the construction of the sermon that needs to be identified.

After these sentences have been shared and discussed, the group moves to other I-statements about the sermon. The preacher's role is listener. As group members discuss the feedback, the preacher may want to ask questions for clarification. The preacher may learn what helped the sermon and what hindered its being heard as intended, and in the discussion the preacher may experiment *briefly* with how an identified problem might be corrected. The preacher should not, however, take time to defend what he or she had in mind or the rationale for the sermon's construction. Some preachers like to talk so much that they inadvertently find themselves preaching their sermons again. Such behavior may discourage the group from giving feedback. The result is that the purpose of the session is damaged.

As the conversation slows down or seems to be completed, the preacher may want to ask questions about specific moments in the sermon. The preacher may have had difficulty in crafting one specific part of the sermon or may have experimented with some new strategy. The preacher may want to request feedback to assess moments of that kind in the sermon.

The group may sense the appropriate time for ending the conversation and moving to closure. The group will do well to have set a definite ending time before the session began and to end at that time unless there is a mutual agreement to continue for a specified number of minutes. The group will do well to have in mind, however, that the longer the session lasts, the more scattered and less accurate the feedback becomes. The group, led by its facilitator, should be sure to adjourn before everyone begins to abandon disciplined feedback and to rewrite the sermon to his or her own satisfaction.

ABOUT FEEDBACK SHEETS

The urgency of using feedback sheets is covered above. Sample sheets adapted from their use in seminary homiletics classes are included at the end of this Appendix. However, perhaps using these samples as guides, the preacher or the preacher together with the listening group may want to design their own feedback sheet, accommodating the special style or method used by the preacher and the special interests and concerns of the group members.

After a given feedback sheet has been used for several sessions, the group will discover omissions that should be covered or questions that are not useful. Redesigning the sheet from time to time is appropriate.

Appendix D

SAMPLE FEEDBACK SHEET A

Form for Evaluation of Classroom Sermons

Preacher _____

Listener _____

Date _____

Please respond to the questions that best help you to give feedback to the preacher. Use the reverse side of the page as needed.

Write in one sentence what you heard the central point of the sermon to be.

What portion(s) of the scripture did you hear emphasized in the exegesis?

What did the sermon say to help its central point be relevant to the listeners?

Circle the word below that best reports the extent to which you sense yourself involved in the human dilemma the sermon spoke about.

not involved at all	some- what involved	involved	very involved	extremely involved
1	2	3	4	5

What elements of the sermon contributed to its being effective?

How did the language of the sermon help/hinder your listening and understanding?

How did any stories, images, or illustrations help/hinder your understanding?

How did the preacher's delivery help/hinder your listening and understanding?

What might the preacher do to present a more effective sermon next time?

SAMPLE FEEDBACK SHEET B

Form for Evaluation of Classroom Sermons

Preacher _____
Listener _____
Date _____

Write in one sentence what you heard the central point of the sermon to be.

Circle any adjectives or descriptive phrases that describe your personal responses to the sermon.

The outline of the sermon was:

> clear
> helpful
> confusing
> too complicated
> vague
> repetitious

Other:_____

The scripture used was:

> clear
> helpful
> too much
> not enough
> supported the point being made
> complicated
> not connected to the point
> confusing
> interesting
> compelling

Other: _____

The point of the sermon was:

> related to my life
> unrelated to me
> O.K.
> somewhat helpful
> very helpful
> interestingly presented
> overstated
> fresh and new
> worn out

Other: _____

The preacher's language was:

> inspiring
> repetitious
> lofty
> simple
> unpersuasive
> persuasive
> rambling
> precise
> obtuse
> flamboyant
> ungrammatical
> drawn out

Other: _____

The preacher's delivery was:

> clear
> well-paced
> good volume
> too loud
> inaudible
> occasionally inaudible
> persuasive
> engaging
> off-putting
> distracting
> moving
> effective
> well-prepared
> fluent
> halting appropriate

Other: _____

The preacher's stories/illustrations/metaphors were:

> interesting
> artfully crafted
> confusing
> distracting
> helpful

Other: _____

Write on the back of the page what the preacher may do to make his/her sermon and its delivery more effective next time.

SAMPLE FEEDBACK SHEET C

Preacher _____
Listener _____
Date _____

(*Use the reverse side of the page or additional pages as needed.*)

Write in one sentence what you heard the central point of the sermon to be.

What other information unrelated to the central point did you hear?

To what extent did you sense yourself involved in the sermon? Mark a point on the scale that best represents your answer.

not at all involved	slightly involved	fairly involved	involved	very involved
1	2	3	4	5

How did the preacher's language and word choice help or hinder?

How did any stories, images, or illustrations help or hinder your listening and understanding?

How did the verbal or physical aspects of the delivery help or hinder your listening and understanding?

What elements of the sermon contributed to its being effective?

What might the preacher do to present a more effective sermon next time?

A QUOTATION ABOUT SERMON CRITIQUE

The quotation below, written by an author discussing homiletical method, is one of the best summaries available of what the sermon evaluation process is about. It is available here for discussion by the listening group and their preacher before they begin and perhaps from time to time as they work together week by week.

> When people are asked to critique preaching they have heard, reliably they usually report quite similar things. For instance, to the question, "What has caused bad preaching you have heard to be bad?" people will typically respond that bad homilies are bad because they don't deliver one simple message; ramble on and on; are either too abstract or too simple; are non-scriptural; don't relate to real life issues; emerge only out of the preacher's interests, ideologies, or life issues; have too many unrelated points; don't suggest a plan of action. Conversely, when pressed to identify those features which have made good preaching effective, people often reply that good homilies are good because they are to the point; address issues of critical importance to the lives of hearers; are scriptural; suggest a mission or plan of action as a result of the homily; feature a disciplined and reasonable use of time and end when they are finished.[3]

3. Monshua, *Preaching*, 24–25.

Appendix E

A SERMON BY WILLIAM HETHCOCK[1]

A Sermon Preached at Otey Memorial Church, Sewanee

THE FIRST SUNDAY AFTER THE EPIPHANY:
THE BAPTISM OF OUR LORD
MARK 1:4–11
JANUARY 11, 2009

> *John the baptizer appeared in the wilderness, proclaiming a baptism of repentance for the forgiveness of sins. And people from the whole Judean countryside and all the people of Jerusalem were going out to him, and were baptized by him in the river Jordan, confessing their sins. Now John was clothed with camel's hair, with a leather belt around his waist, and he ate locusts and wild honey. He proclaimed, "The one who is more powerful than I is coming after me; I am not worthy to stoop down and untie the thong of his sandals. I have baptized you with water; but he will baptize you with the Holy Spirit."*
>
> *In those days Jesus came from Nazareth of Galilee and was baptized by John in the Jordan. And just as he was coming up out of the water, he saw the heavens torn apart and the Spirit descending like a dove on him. And a voice came from heaven, "You are my Son, the Beloved; with you I am well pleased."*

FOCUS SENTENCE: The baptism we have received is meant to enable us to be disciples of Jesus Christ.

---

1. William Hethcock, Professor of Homiletics, Emeritus, The School of Theology, University of the South, Sewanee, Tennessee.

I

A wonderful long-running Broadway comedy play,
  comes to my mind this morning.

  It's "Life with Father,"
    which became a movie in 1947.

    The reason I'm thinking of it
      is
        that the secondary,
          if not the primary,
            theme of the story
              is Holy Baptism.

I think of the movie today
  because today is

The Feast of the Baptism of Our Lord
    remembering Mark's story of John the Baptist
      baptizing Jesus
        at John's wilderness place
          on the Jordan River.

  The gospel reading today
    and that sixty-year-old movie
      both raise the question,
        "What does holy baptism mean
          in the Christian Church?"
The setting of the movie
  is
    New York City in 1883.
Clarence Day,
  a wealthy Wall Street financier,
    has a wife and four children,
      all boys,
        whom he attempts
          to control and manage
      with the same meticulous
        precision and rules
          he uses at the office.

He presents himself outwardly
   as a strong, domineering father,
      who is actually fairly much manipulated
         by his wife and sons.

   The family are Episcopalians,
      which is required to make the story funny.

   We all know that Episcopalians are funny.

For Clarence's wife Vinnie,
   it's a matter of faith.

   For Clarence himself,
      being an Episcopalian
         is the decent and proper thing to do.

One night at dinner,
   Clarence casually mentions
      that he has never been baptized.

His wife Vinnie is shocked and appalled.

   She initiates one plot after another
      to get Clarence to correct this dreadful fault.

   Vinnie tells her husband
      that he is not a Christian.

      She explains over and over,
         as do the children,
            that a person never baptized
               will surely go to hell
and burn in unquenchable fire
   forever.
   Further,
      Clarence and she
         will not be together in heaven,
            which pains her greatly.

> Vinnie explains that
>> she misses him dreadfully
>>> even when he just goes to Ohio.

> So she must get Clarence baptized.

Clarence, of course,
> cannot submit to the baptism he missed as a child.

He thinks it would be humiliating.

> "Baptism is all right for children,"
> he shouts,
>> "but it's too late to correct it now."

> He goes on to bellow,
>> "They can't keep me out of heaven
>>> on a technicality."

And the complaining continues
> all the way to the church
>> on the day Vinnie has finally arranged
>>> for Clarence to be baptized.

II

The meaning of baptism
> in this funny play
>> is far from what we are hearing
>>> in Mark
>>>> this morning.

John is at his wilderness place
> "proclaiming a baptism
>> of repentance for the forgiveness of sins."

He is there in the wilderness place
  he has chosen
    for his ministry,
      and men and women
        are coming from the towns and villages
  as well as Jerusalem
    to hear his preaching.

John is baptizing people,
  and he is very clear about
    what his baptism means.

His baptism is
  "a baptism of repentance
    for the forgiveness of sins."

If a person were willing
  to ask God's forgiveness
    with sincerity and truth,
      that repentance,
        he assures everyone,
      will bring God's forgiveness.

If a person can do that,
  John then leads that man or woman
    into the waters of the Jordan River
    and washes that person
      as a sign of
        new spiritual cleanness.

  This baptism
    makes a person's outside clean
as a sign of
  that person's new inner clean-ness.

But remember John the Baptist's main job.

Mark relates
> that John is in the wilderness
>> preparing the way
>>> for the coming of the Lord Jesus the Christ.

> And John preaches strongly
>> that the baptism Jesus initiates
>>> will be greater than his.

> Jesus will bring a new dimension
>> to John's own baptism.

>> Jesus
>>> when he comes
>>>> will baptize the people
>>>>> with the Holy Spirit.

>>> Something is going to happen
> to and for the person
>> who is baptized,
>>> according to Jesus,
>>>> and that something,
>>> the gift of the Holy Spirit,
>>>> adds to the person's
>>>>> repentance and forgiveness.

Men and women receiving Jesus' baptism are filled with
> and strengthened by
>>> the presence of the Holy Spirit
>>>> within them.

When Jesus comes to John's wilderness place,
> he allows John to baptize him,
>> but not because Jesus needs
>>> repentance and forgiveness.

What Jesus is doing
　　as he allows John to baptize him
　　　　that day
　　　　　　is actually
　　　　　　　　acting out
　　　　　　　　　　what he wants us to know.

　　When you and I were baptized,
　　　　we entered into
　　　　　　a close and intimate relationship
　　　　　　　　with Jesus as
　　　　　　　　　　our Lord.

　　We became a part of Jesus' body,
　　　　the church.

　　　　Jesus' entering into the water
　　　　　　prefigures his own death,
　　and his coming out of the water
　　prefigures his own resurrection.
　　　　So that you and I,
　　　　　　when we are baptized,
　　　　　　　　enter into Jesus' death with him—
　　　　　　　　　　we die with him—
and we come away from the water receiving a new life
　　　　　　　　　　according to
　　　　　　　　　　　　Jesus' resurrection.

　　　　You and I
　　　　　　in our baptism
　　　　　　　　die a death to sin,
　　　　　　　　　　and we are raised with Jesus
　　　　　　　　　　　　in his own new resurrected life.

Our understanding of baptism
　　is
　　　　that it's about life in the world here and now.

When we are baptized,
    even as infants,
        God acts to fill us
            with the Spirit
                that will protect us.

That same Spirit
    enables us to resist evil
        and to accomplish the good
            God calls us to do,
    to become disciples of Jesus Christ.

Baptism is not about saving us from hell,
    though Vinnie Day
    has good company
        among Christians
            in the mistaken belief
                she argues
                    with her husband
                        Clarence.

In 2007,
    the Roman Catholic church,
        speaking on this subject,
            agreed
                that we must trust in God's mercy
to act in behalf of those not baptized,
            which is akin to what
                Episcopalians and other Anglicans
                    have been thinking
                        all along.

Baptism is not intended
    to prevent something dreadful,
        but to enable something
            that is very good.

III

There is a story,
  perhaps apocryphal,
    that I heard recently.

  Some decades ago,
    before automobiles
      came to be manufactured largely by robots,
        assembly line workers
          amassed a wide variety of tools
            in their home workshops.
These were tools
    they had simply brought home
      from the factory
        and never returned.

    As the story goes,
      the practice was widespread
        at the Ford Motor Company,
          and management
            seemed unable
              to do anything about it.

It happened that one employee
  was deciding
    to become a member
      of a Christian church,
        and as he moved toward
          this church membership decision,
            he was also to be baptized.

  As he learned more and more
    about the baptism he was to receive
      and what it would mean,
        the presence of the tool collection
          in his garage
            began to weigh on his mind.

>   He decided
>   that as a Christian
>   he must take all the tools
>   and return them
>   to the Ford factory.
>
> When he handed the tools over to his foreman,
>   he explained that
>   in good conscience
>   he could not keep them.
>
> As a newly baptized Christian,
>   he had to return the tools
>   to where they belonged.
>
> Word went up through management,
>   and a cable was sent
>   to Mr. Henry Ford,
>   who was in Europe at the time.
>
>   Ford learned
>   that an employee
>   had returned to the auto plant
>   all his stolen tools
>   because he was about to become
>   a baptized Christian.
>
>   Ford is said to have shot back a cable
>   right away
>   saying,
>   "Dam up the Detroit River
>   and baptize the whole lot of them."

IV

We all know something
   of Mr. Ford's genius.

But if this story is true,
   we have to conclude
      that he wasn't so sharp
         when it comes to a theology of baptism.

And he's not the only one.

   We don't force baptism on people
      as Vinnie Day was trying to do
         to her husband, Clarence.

   There is an atmosphere in our church
      that sometimes tends to emphasize
         a social dimension of baptism,
           a big family event
              surrounding,
as some Britishers sometimes say,
   having the baby "done."
The reading today
   about John baptizing Jesus
      gives us a reason
         to look at baptism
           again.

The factory worker is the one who got the point.
   He seemed to understand
      that being baptized
         required a change,
           and perhaps he understood
              that he was being strengthened
                 to make a change
                    for the good.

He was being enabled
   to become
      a disciple of Jesus Christ.

V

You and I have been baptized.
  It's entirely possible for us
    to forget about it,
      especially since it may have happened
        for us
          when we were infants,
    before we had conscious knowledge
      of what was going on.

But the truth is,
  according to today's gospel story,
    at the time of our baptism,
      God acted to give us
        what we need
          to become his faithful disciples.
  Regardless of when we were baptized,
    we have been given the gift
      of being strengthened
by the presence of the Holy Spirit of God within us.

We can ignore
    what God has done for us,
      as many do,
        especially those
          whose parents and godparents
            did not fulfill the vow
              made at our baptism
      to see that the child
        they presented was
          "brought up
            in the Christian faith and life."

Or,
> we can respond
>> to the presence of the Holy Spirit,
>>> who has resided within us
>>>> in a special way
>>>>> ever since our baptism.

When we respond to our baptism
> and all that it means,
>> we are enabled
>>> to move toward becoming
>>>> disciples of Jesus,
>>> the disciples of Jesus
>>>> we are called to be.

Bibliography

WORKS BY WILLIAM HETHCOCK

Hethcock, William. "'Crossing the River': Proclaiming Deeper Truth from the Pulpit." In *Simul Justus et Peccator; Essays in Honor of Donald S. Armentrout*, edited by Ralph K. Hawkins, 145–170. Sewanee, TN: University of the South Press, 2003.

———. "Exegesis for Proper 6, Year A." In *Tuesday Morning: Resource for Ministry and Liturgical Preaching* 10 (2, 2008) 27–28.

———. "How Can You Tell When You Are Preaching?" *Papers of the Academy of Homiletics*. Unpublished paper, 1990.

———. Interviews by Jerrilee Parker Lewallen. Sewanee, TN. May 30, 2008; June 4, 2008; June 6, 2008, January 10, 2009.

———. "Invocations and 'Amens.'" In *Tuesday Morning: Resource for Ministry and Liturgical Preaching* 5 (2, 2003) 4–5.

———. "Looking Again at Teaching Homiletics." In *Reconciliation and Healing: Sermons and Comments from the 2007 Preaching Excellence Program*, vol. 16, edited by Timothy J. Mulder and Fred T. Rossi, 92–99. Springfield, NJ: The Preaching Excellence Foundation, 2007.

———. Middler Homiletics. The School of Theology of The University of the South, Sewanee, TN. Jerrilee Parker Lewallen's course notes, 1996–1997.

———. Personal correspondence with Jerrilee Parker Lewallen. July 2008.

———. "Preaching the Kingdom of God in the Synoptic Gospels." In *With Ever Joyful Hearts: Essays on Liturgy and Music Honoring Marion J. Hatchett*, edited by J. Neil Alexander, 163–185. New York: Church Publishing, 1999.

———. "The Sermon as Educational Event." *Sewanee Theological Review* 38 (1, Christmas, 1994) 21–38.

———. *Sermons Preached at Bruton 2000*. Williamsburg, VA: Bruton Parish Episcopal Church, 2000.

———. "'Serving the Word': A Commentary for Proper 28, Year A." In *Homily Service: An Ecumenical Resource for Sharing the Word* 26 (8, 1993) 34–36. This essay is a section within the commentary for November 13, 1993, by Betty Jean Young, John Petrenko, Lisa A. Tarker, and William Hethcock, 25–36.

———. Unpublished Homiletics I (Middler Homiletics) course handouts. The School of Theology of The University of the South, Sewanee, TN, 1996–1997.

———. Unpublished Homiletics I (Middler Homiletics) lecture notes. The School of Theology of The University of the South, Sewanee, TN, 1996–1997.

———. Unpublished Homiletics course handouts. Virginia Theological Seminary, Alexandria, VA, 2004. (These include handout #7, "Your Itch and Scratch Workbook"; and handout #23, "Preaching at the Eucharist: A Talk Presented to the Preaching Excellence Conference, Virginia Seminary, June 5, 2000.")

———. Unpublished Homiletics lecture notes. Virginia Theological Seminary, Alexandria, VA, 2004.

OTHER WORKS CITED

Aland, Kurt, ed. *Synopsis of the Four Gospels*. United Bible Societies and Peabody, MA: Hendrickson, 1982.

Armentrout, Don S. "William Hethcock: An Academic History and Bibliography." *Homiletics: A Festschrift in Honor of William Hethcock. Sewanee Theological Review* 41 (3, Pentecost, 1998) 203–10.

Brueggemann, Walter. "Preaching as Reimagination." In *A Reader on Preaching*, edited by David Day, Jeff Astley, and Leslie J. Francis, 17–29. Burlington, VT: Ashgate, 2005.

Bryan, Christopher. *A Preface to Mark: Notes on the Gospel in Its Literary and Cultural Settings*. New York: Oxford University Press, 1993.

Craddock, Fred B. "Inductive Movement in Preaching." In *As One Without Authority*, rev. ed., 43–62. St. Louis: Chalice, 2001.

———. *Preaching*. Nashville: Abingdon, 1985.

Davis, Henry Grady. *Design for Preaching*. Philadelphia: Muhlenberg, 1958.

Dokoupil, Tony. "Television: Absolution for Couch Potatoes." *Newsweek* (June 2, 2008) 9.

Dunkly, Jim. "Fresh Help for Possibly Stale Greek." *Tuesday Morning: Resource for Ministry and Liturgical Preaching* 10 (2, 2008) 4–5.

Edwards, O. C., Jr. *A History of Preaching*. Nashville: Abingdon, 2004.

———. *The Living and Active Word: One Way to Preach from the Bible Today*. New York: Seabury, 1975.

Hatchett, Marion J. *Commentary on the American Prayer Book*. San Francisco: Harper Collins, 1995.

Holmes, Urban T. III. *A Priest in Community: Exploring the Roots of Ministry*. New York: Seabury, 1978.

Johnson, Luke Timothy. *The Writings of the New Testament*. Philadelphia: Fortress, 1986. (A third edition of this book is now available.)

Jones, William Augustus, Jr. "Introduction." In *Outstanding Black Sermons*, vol. 1, edited by J. Alfred Smith, 6–7. Valley Forge, PA: Judson, 1976.

Jowett, John Henry. *The Preacher, His Life and Work*. New York: Dorana, 1912.

Keizer, Garret. *A Dresser of Sycamore Trees: The Finding of a Ministry*. San Francisco: Harper Collins, 1993.

Kysar, Robert. *John: The Maverick Gospel*. Rev. ed. Louisville, KY: Westminster John Knox Press, 1993. First published 1976, John Knox. Page references are to the 1993 edition.

Long, Thomas G. *The Witness of Preaching*. Louisville: Westminster John Knox, 1989.

Lowry, Eugene L. *The Homiletical Plot: The Sermon as Narrative Art Form*. Expanded ed. Louisville: Westminster John Knox Press, 2000. First published 1980, John Knox. Page references are to the 2000 edition.

———. *How to Preach a Parable: Designs for Narrative Sermons*. Nashville: Abingdon, 1989.

Marshall, Peter. *Mr. Jones, Meet the Master: Sermons and Prayers of Peter Marshall*. With a Preface and Introduction by Catherine Marshall. Boston: G. K. Hall, 1973.

Monshua, Michael. O. P., ed. *Preaching at the Double Feast, Homiletics for Eucharistic Worship*. Collegeville, MN: Liturgical Press, 2006.

Müller, Morgan. "Son of Man." In *The Oxford Companion to the Bible*, edited by Bruce M. Metzger and Michael D. Coogan, 711–713. New York: Oxford University Press, 1993.

Nickle, Keith F. *The Synoptic Gospels: An Introduction*. Atlanta: John Knox, 1980.

Perkins, Pheme. "The Gospel of Mark." In *The New Interpreter's Bible: A Commentary in Twelve Volumes*, edited by Leander Keck, 508–733. Nashville: Abingdon, 1995.

Peterson, Eugene H. *The Message: The New Testament in Contemporary Language*. Colorado Springs: Navpress, 1993.

Rice, Charles. "Shaping Sermons by the Interplay of Text and Metaphor." In *Preaching Biblically*, edited by Don M. Wardlaw, 101–20. Philadelphia: Westminster, 1983.

Rienecker, Fritz. *Linguistic Key to the Greek New Testament*, edited by Cleo L. Rogers, Jr. Grand Rapids, MI: Zondervan, 1976.

Smith, Albert Richard. Remarks in Beginning Greek I and II lectures. The School of Theology at The University of the South, Sewanee, TN., 1995–1996. Personal communication, February 3, 2009.

Stambaugh, John E., and David L. Balch. *The New Testament in Its Social Environment*. Philadelphia: Westminster, 1986.

Taylor, Barbara Brown. *Gospel Medicine*. Boston: Cowley, 1995.

———. *The Luminous Web: Essays on Science and Religion*. Cambridge, MA: Cowley, 2000.

———. *The Preaching Life*. Boston: Cowley, 1993.

———. *The Seeds of Heaven*. Cincinnati: Forward Movement, 1990.

———. *Teaching Sermons on Suffering: God in Pain*, edited by Ronald J. Allen. The Teaching Sermon Series. Nashville: Abingdon, 1998.

Turrell, James F. Unpublished sermon delivered at All Saint's Chapel, Sewanee, TN, June 1, 2008.

Wilson, Paul Scott. *The Four Pages of the Sermon: A Guide to Biblical Preaching*. Nashville: Abingdon, 1999.

Wright, N. T. *The New Testament and the People of God*. Minneapolis: Fortress, 1992.

———. *What Saint Paul Really Said: Was Paul of Tarsus the Real Founder of Christianity?* Grand Rapids, MI: Eerdmans; Cincinnati, OH: Forward Movement, 1997.

Wright, Rebecca Abts. Remarks in Old Testament: Foundations I and II lectures. The School of Theology at The University of the South, Sewanee, TN, 1995–1996.

www.ingramcontent.com/pod-product-compliance
Lightning Source LLC
Chambersburg PA
CBHW070918180426

43192CB00038B/1748